OUR BEST

CAST-IRON COOKING

RECIPES

To cooks everywhere who want to create easy & delicious meals using their favorite cast-iron cookware.

Gooseberry Patch
An imprint of Globe Pequot
64 S. Main Street
Essex, CT 06426

www.gooseberrypatch.com
1 800 854 6673

Copyright, 2022
Gooseberry Patch
978-1-62093-499-9

• • • • • • • • • • • • • • • • • • • •

Do you have a tried & true recipe... tip, craft or memory that you'd like to see featured in a **Gooseberry Patch** cookbook? Visit our website at **www.gooseberrypatch.com** and follow the easy steps to submit your favorite family recipe.

Or send them to us at:
Gooseberry Patch
PO Box 812
Columbus, OH 43216-0812

Don't forget to include the number of servings your recipe makes, plus your name, address, phone number and email address. If we select your recipe, your name will appear right along with it... and you'll receive a FREE copy of the book!

CONTENTS

For the Love of Cast Iron

We all remember watching our mothers, dads and grandparents cooking with a favorite pan. It was a seasoned cast-iron wonder that could cook on top of the stove or in the oven and transformed a simple recipe into a mouthwatering meal. That humble, heavy-duty pan did double duty indeed. Today there are dozens of cast-iron pans available that you can use to create your own amazing recipes.

About Cast Iron:
Cast-iron cookware was first produced in the mid 1800s and was especially popular among homemakers during the first half of the 20th century. It was an inexpensive yet very durable cookware. Every American kitchen had to have at least one cast-iron skillet in their cupboard. It fried, baked and held the heat like no other pan.

Special Abilities:
Cast iron's ability to handle and maintain very high cooking temperatures makes it a great choice for searing or frying. Because it has excellent heat retention, it is a great option for stews and soups. It also keeps foods warm for a long time after the cooking is done. Cast-iron pans are also an excellent choice for baking cornbreads, cakes and cobblers.

Seasoning:

Seasoning or curing cast-iron pans is the process of coating the surface with heated fat or oil. The item is thoroughly cleaned, then coated in a very thin layer of fat or oil, and then heated beyond the smoke point. This produces a resistant hard coating that helps prevents sticking. Most new cast-iron pans have instructions from the manufacturer on the best way to season the pans. Some cast-iron cookware is pre-seasoned by manufacturers, but most pans need to be seasoned by the users. Without seasoning, the pan will rust rapidly after cleaning.

Cleaning:

Cast-iron cookware should not be cleaned like other cookware. Do not put it in the dishwasher because it can remove the seasoning and cause rusting. You can hand wash it with just a mild soap and dry it immediately, then reseason as needed. You can also use coarse salt and a soft rag to clean the pan.

Enameled Cast Iron:

Enameled cast iron is cast iron that has an enamel glaze applied to the surface. Adding the glaze with the cast iron prevents rusting, eliminates the need to season the iron and makes it easier to clean. Enamel pans make excellent Dutch ovens where slow cooking is often used. It is more expensive than bare cast-iron pans, but the beautiful colors that come from the fusion of the enamel glaze with the iron make the pans excellent serving dishes right from the stove. Care should be given to any enameled cast-iron pan because the enamel coating can chip if the pans are not handled appropriately.

Savory Zucchini Frittata, p. 26

CHAPTER ONE

HEARTY
Breakfasts

Blackberry Skillet Pancake, p. 32

Baked Eggs in Tomatoes, p. 10

Wendy Paffenroth, Pine Island, NY

Apple-Stuffed French Toast

We love to make this recipe for breakfast because we love both apples and French Toast.

Makes 4 servings

3 apples, peeled, cored and diced
2 T. brown sugar, packed
cinnamon to taste
2 eggs, beaten
1/2 c. 2% milk
1 t. vanilla extract
8 slices whole-wheat bread
2 t. powdered sugar

In a microwave-safe bowl, combine apples, brown sugar and cinnamon. Cover and microwave on high for 5 minutes. In a separate bowl, stir together eggs, milk and vanilla. Spray a cast-iron frying pan with non-stick vegetable spray and heat over medium heat. Quickly dip the bread on both sides in the egg mixture and place in pan. Cook until golden on both sides. To serve, put a scoop of the apple mixture in the middle. Dust with powdered sugar.

Vickie, Gooseberry Patch

Cheesy Hashbrown Nuggets

Yum! These are always welcome on a brunch or breakfast buffet. Swap in your favorite cheese, if you like.

Makes about 2 dozen

6 slices bacon
1 egg, beaten
1/2 c. sour cream
salt and pepper to taste
1-1/2 c. shredded sharp Cheddar
   cheese
20-oz. pkg. frozen shredded
   hashbrowns, thawed

Cook bacon in a cast-iron skillet over medium heat until crisp. Drain; set aside bacon on paper towels. In a bowl, whisk together egg, sour cream and seasonings; stir in cheese. Fold in hashbrowns and bacon. Scoop a heaping tablespoon of hashbrown mixture and make a ball. Add mixture to well-greased mini muffin cups by heaping tablespoonfuls. Bake at 425 degrees for 20 minutes, or until hot and golden. Serve warm.

DID YOU KNOW?
Cast-iron pans come in many shapes and sizes. Skillets and Dutch ovens are the best known, but you can also find muffin pans, bread pans, popover pans and more.

Cheesy Hashbrown Nuggets

Suzanne Fritz, Hutto, TX

Ham & Potato Skillet

This is a versatile dish that we sometimes eat for breakfast too. It's so good topped with a dash of hot sauce, picante sauce or sour cream.

Serves 6

4-1/2 t. butter
3 baking potatoes, peeled and thinly
  sliced
1/2 onion, chopped
1/2 green pepper, chopped
2 c. cooked ham, diced
salt and pepper to taste
3 eggs, lightly beaten
1/2 c. shredded Cheddar cheese

Melt butter in a large cast-iron skillet over medium heat. Layer half each of the potatoes, onion, green pepper and ham in skillet. Repeat layers; season with salt and pepper. Cover and cook for 10 to 15 minutes, until potatoes are tender. Pour eggs over potato mixture; cover and cook for 3 to 5 minutes, until eggs are almost set. Sprinkle cheese over all. Remove from heat; cover and let stand until cheese is melted. Cut into wedges to serve.

Jill Burton, Gooseberry Patch

Baked Eggs in Tomatoes

So pretty for a brunch...a delicious way to enjoy tomatoes from the farmers' market.

Serves 6

6 tomatoes, tops cut off
1/4 t. pepper
1/2 c. corn, thawed if frozen
1/2 c. red pepper, diced
1/2 c. mushrooms, diced
2 T. cream cheese, softened and
  divided
6 eggs, beaten
2 t. fresh chives, minced
1/4 c. grated Parmesan cheese

With a spoon, carefully scoop out each tomato, creating shells. Sprinkle pepper inside tomatoes. Divide corn, red pepper and mushrooms among tomatoes; top each with one teaspoon cream cheese. In a bowl, whisk together eggs and chives. Divide egg mixture among tomatoes; top with Parmesan cheese. Place filled tomatoes in a lightly greased cast-iron skillet. Bake, uncovered, at 350 degrees until egg mixture is set, about 45 to 50 minutes. Serve warm.

Baked Eggs in Tomatoes

Vickie, Gooseberry Patch

Black Bean Breakfast Bowls

We love to serve this dish for breakfast on weekends. It looks so special...and tastes so yummy!

Serves 2

2 T. olive oil
4 eggs, beaten
15-1/2-oz. can black beans, drained
   and rinsed
1 avocado, peeled, pitted and sliced
1/4 c. shredded Cheddar cheese
1/4 c. favorite salsa
salt and pepper to taste

Heat oil in a cast-iron skillet over medium heat. Add eggs and scramble as desired, 3 to 5 minutes; remove from heat. Place beans in a microwave-safe bowl. Microwave on high until warm, one to 2 minutes. To serve, divide into bowls; top each bowl with eggs, avocado, cheese and salsa. Season with salt and pepper.

Jo Ann, Gooseberry Patch

Jo Ann's Garden Frittata

Family & friends are sure to love this savory egg dish. It's filled with brightly colored vegetables...beautiful to look at and delicious to eat.

Makes 8 servings

4 thick slices bacon, chopped
1 onion, diced
1 red pepper, thinly sliced
1 c. corn
1 c. green beans, thinly sliced
1 bunch Swiss chard, thinly sliced
3 eggs, beaten
1-1/4 c. half-and-half
1/8 t. dried thyme
salt and pepper to taste
1 c. shredded Cheddar cheese

In a large cast-iron skillet over medium-high heat, cook bacon until crisp. Drain bacon on paper towels; reserve drippings. In one tablespoon drippings, sauté onion, red pepper and corn for 5 minutes. Add beans; sauté another 3 minutes. Transfer vegetable mixture to a bowl; set aside. Add one teaspoon drippings to skillet; sauté chard for 2 minutes. Add to vegetable mixture in bowl. In a separate large bowl, whisk eggs, half-and-half and seasonings. Stir in bacon, cheese and vegetable mixture; pour into skillet. Bake at 375 degrees for about 35 minutes, until set and crust is golden. Let stand for about 10 minutes; cut into squares.

Jo Ann's Garden Frittata

Deborah Wells, Broken Arrow, OK

Cheese & Chive Scrambled Eggs

Paired with hot biscuits, this makes a great breakfast for any day of the week!

Serves 2 to 3

6 eggs, beaten
1/4 t. lemon pepper
1 T. fresh chives, chopped
1/8 t. salt
1 T. butter
1/3 c. shredded Colby Jack cheese
1/3 c. cream cheese, softened

In a bowl, combine eggs, pepper, chives and salt; set aside. Melt butter in a cast-iron skillet over medium-low heat; add egg mixture. Stir to scramble, cooking until set. Remove from heat; stir in cheeses until melted.

Jill Ball, Highland, UT

Hearty Breakfast Quinoa

I'm always looking for hearty, healthy, yummy breakfast ideas. This one is great! My family likes it, and I feel good that they're starting the day right.

Makes 6 servings

1 c. skim milk
1 c. water
1/4 t. salt
1 c. quinoa, uncooked and rinsed
1 t. cinnamon

2 c. blueberries or raspberries, thawed if frozen
1/3 c. chopped toasted walnuts
1 T. unsweetened flaked coconut

In a Dutch oven over medium heat, stir together milk, water, salt and quinoa. Bring to a boil. Reduce heat to medium-low; cover and cook for 15 minutes, or until quinoa is tender and liquid is absorbed. Remove from heat; let stand, covered, for about 5 minutes. Gently stir in cinnamon and berries. Just before serving, top with walnuts and coconut.

Jody Pressley, Charlotte, NC

Bran & Raisin Muffins

These bran muffins are an all-time favorite with just about everyone!

Makes one dozen, serves 12

2 c. bran & raisin cereal
1-1/2 c. milk
1-1/2 c. all-purpose flour
1 t. baking soda
1/4 t. salt
2 eggs, beaten
1/2 c. brown sugar, packed
2 T. butter, melted

Mix cereal with milk; set aside. In a large bowl, combine remaining ingredients; stir in cereal mixture. Fill greased cast-iron muffin cups about 2/3 full with batter. Bake at 350 degrees for 15 to 20 minutes.

Bran & Raisin Muffins

Mary Mayall, Dracut, MA

No-Crust Spinach Quiche

If you want meat in this dish, add chopped ham or crumbled bacon to this delicious crustless quiche.

Serves 6

10-oz. pkg. frozen chopped spinach,
    thawed and drained
1 T. chopped chives
1/2 c. mushrooms, chopped
6 eggs, beaten
1/2 c. milk
1 c. shredded Swiss or Cheddar
    cheese

Spread spinach in a greased 9" cast-iron pan or pie plate. Sprinkle chives and/or mushrooms on top, if desired. Beat together eggs and milk; stir in cheese. Pour egg mixture evenly over spinach. Bake at 350 degrees for 25 to 35 minutes, until top is golden and a knife tip inserted into center comes out clean. Cool slightly before cutting.

Gail Blain, Grand Island, NE

Nutty Skillet Granola

Fill small bags with this easy-to-fix granola...perfect for grab & go breakfasts and snacks.

Makes about 7 cups

1 c. quick-cooking oats, uncooked
1 c. old-fashioned oats, uncooked
1 c. sliced almonds
1/2 c. chopped walnuts
1/2 c. chopped pecans
1/2 c. wheat germ
1/4 c. oil
1/2 c. maple syrup
3/4 c. light brown sugar, packed
1 c. raisins

In a large bowl, mix oats, nuts and wheat germ; set aside. In a large cast-iron skillet over medium heat, combine oil, maple syrup and brown sugar. Cook, stirring constantly, until brown sugar melts and mixture just begins to bubble, about 3 minutes. Add oat mixture; stir well to coat completely. Reduce heat to medium-low. Cook, stirring occasionally, until mixture begins to sizzle and toast, about 3 to 4 minutes; be careful not to burn. Remove from heat; stir in raisins. Cool for 10 minutes; transfer to an airtight container. Will keep for up to 2 weeks.

Nutty Skillet Granola

Virginia Watson, Scranton, PA

Grandma's Warm Breakfast Fruit

This delectable fruit compote is delicious served warm with any egg dish.

Serves 6 to 8

3 apples, peeled, cored and thickly
   sliced
1 orange, peeled and sectioned
3/4 c. raisins
1/2 c. dried plums, chopped
3 c. plus 3 T. water, divided
1/2 c. sugar
1/2 t. cinnamon
2 T. cornstarch
Garnish: favorite granola

Combine fruit and 3 cups water in a cast-iron skillet over medium heat. Bring to a boil; reduce heat and simmer for 10 minutes. Stir in sugar and cinnamon. In a small bowl, mix together cornstarch and remaining water; stir into fruit mixture. Bring to a boil, stirring constantly; cook and stir for 2 minutes. Spoon into bowls; top with granola to serve.

Tonya Sheppard, Galveston, TX

Huevos Rancheros to Go-Go

Serve these eggs with sliced fresh avocado for a deliciously different breakfast.

Makes 4 servings

2 c. red or green tomatillo salsa
4 eggs
4 8-inch corn tortillas
1-1/4 c. shredded Monterey Jack
   cheese or crumbled queso fresco

Lightly grease a cast-iron skillet; place over medium heat. Pour salsa into skillet; bring to a simmer. With a spoon, make 4 wells in salsa. Crack an egg into each well, taking care not to break the yolks. Reduce heat to low; cover and poach eggs for 3 minutes. Remove skillet from heat. Transfer each egg and a scoop of salsa to a tortilla; roll up. Sprinkle with cheese.

Huevos Rancheros to Go-Go

Kathryn Harris, Lufkin, TX

Fiesta Cornbread

If you'd like, shred Pepper Jack cheese and substitute for the Cheddar...it will add more kick. This gets breakfast off to a spicy start!

Serves 6 to 8

1 c. cornmeal
1 c. buttermilk
8-oz. can creamed corn
2 jalapeño peppers, chopped
1/2 t. salt
3/4 t. baking soda
2 eggs, beaten
1 onion, chopped
1/4 c. oil
1 c. shredded Cheddar cheese, divided

Combine first 8 ingredients; set aside. Heat oil in an 8" to 10" cast-iron skillet; pour in half the batter. Sprinkle with half the cheese; pour remaining batter over top. Sprinkle with remaining cheese; bake at 400 degrees for 30 minutes.

Amy Butcher, Columbus, GA

Pesto & Green Onion Omelet

Preserve the fresh herb flavors of summer...make your own pesto sauce to fill this yummy omelet. It's easy!

Makes 3 servings

2 t. canola oil
4 whole eggs
4 egg whites
1/8 t. salt
1/8 t. pepper
2 T. water
1/4 c. green onions, chopped
1 T. pesto sauce
Garnish: green onion tops, cherry
    tomatoes, parsley

Add oil to a cast-iron skillet over medium heat, coating sides and bottom well. Combine eggs and egg whites. Beat until frothy. Stir in salt, pepper, water and onions. Add mixture to hot skillet, and cook without stirring, lifting edges to allow uncooked egg to flow underneath. When almost set, spoon pesto sauce on half of omelet. Fold other half over, slide onto a plate and garnish with green onion tops, tomatoes and parsley. Cut into 3 sections.

Pesto & Green Onion Omelet

Holly Jackson, St George, UT

Ham & Feta Cheese Omelet

This omelet is so simple to make, it will become your go-to-breakfast!

Serves one

2 eggs, beaten
1/4 c. crumbled feta cheese
1/4 c. cucumber, diced
2 T. green onion, chopped
1/4 c. cooked ham, cubed
salt and pepper to taste
Garnish: salsa

Combine all ingredients except salsa in a bowl; mix well. Pour into a lightly greased cast-iron skillet. Without stirring, cook over low heat until set. Fold over; transfer to serving plate. Serve with salsa.

Paula Johnson, Center City, MN

Cinnamon-Pumpkin Pancakes

A great way to enjoy the spicy taste of pumpkin year 'round.

Makes 2 dozen, serves 6

1 c. whole-wheat flour
1 T. sugar
2 t. baking powder
1/4 t. salt
1/2 t. cinnamon
1 c. skim milk
1/2 c. canned pumpkin
2 eggs, separated and divided
1-1/2 T. oil

In a large mixing bowl, combine flour, sugar, baking powder, salt and cinnamon. In a separate bowl, blend together milk, pumpkin, beaten egg yolks and oil. Add pumpkin mixture to flour mixture all at once, stirring until just blended. Beat egg whites until stiff peaks form, then gently fold into pancake batter. Spoon 2 to 3 tablespoons batter onto a cast-iron griddle or skillet sprayed with non-stick vegetable spray. Cook until bubbles begin to form around edges; turn and cook until second side is golden.

Cinnamon-Pumpkin Pancakes

Leianna Logan, Toledo, OH

Sunday Skillet Hash

This is a traditional meat-and-potatoes morning meal you'll want to have again and again! We usually have it for breakfast, but add a fruit or lettuce salad and you have a meal for any time of day.

Serves 4

1 lb. ground pork sausage
2 lbs. potatoes, peeled and diced
1 onion, finely chopped
1 green pepper, finely chopped
salt and pepper to taste

Brown sausage in a large cast-iron skillet; drain drippings. Stir in potatoes, onion and green pepper. Sprinkle with salt and pepper as desired. Cover and reduce heat to medium-low. Cook for 15 minutes or until potatoes are fork-tender.

FLAVOR BOOST
Add a tablespoon of your favorite diced hot pepper or green chilies to give this hash a little kick.

Linda Picard, Newport, OR

Savory Oatmeal Bowls with Egg, Bacon & Kale

This one-bowl breakfast will give you a jump-start for a busy day at school or work.

Serves 2

2 slices bacon, diced
1 bunch kale, thinly sliced
1/2 c. tomato, diced
1 t. red wine vinegar
1/8 t. salt
1 c. cooked steel-cut oats
1/3 c. avocado, peeled, pitted
    and diced
1 t. olive oil
2 eggs
1/8 t. pepper
Optional: 1/2 t. hot pepper sauce

In a large cast-iron skillet over medium heat, cook bacon until almost crisp, stirring occasionally. Add kale; cook for 2 to 4 minutes, until wilted. Stir in tomato, vinegar and salt. Divide oats evenly between 2 bowls. Top with kale mixture and avocado; set aside. Wipe skillet clean with a paper towel; return to medium heat. Add oil and swirl to coat. Crack eggs into skillet, one at a time; cook for 2 minutes. Cover and cook for one minute, or until whites are set. Top each bowl with one egg. Sprinkle with pepper and hot sauce, if using.

Savory Oatmeal Bowls with Egg, Bacon & Kale

Jennifer Howard, Santa Fe, NM

Best-Ever Brunch Potatoes

Eggs, crispy bacon, golden potatoes... just add a basket of fruit muffins and breakfast is served.

Serves 6 to 8

8 slices bacon
3 T. olive oil
2-1/2 lbs. redskin potatoes, diced
8 eggs, beaten
1 t. salt
1/2 T. pepper
3/4 c. sour cream French onion dip
3/4 c. shredded sharp Cheddar
 cheese
1/2 c. green onions, chopped

In a cast-iron skillet over medium-high heat, cook bacon until crisp. Remove bacon to paper towels. Drain skillet; add oil and fry potatoes until tender. In a separate lightly greased skillet, scramble eggs until fluffy; season with salt and pepper. Fold crumbled bacon, dip and cheese into potatoes; stir in scrambled eggs. Sprinkle green onions over top.

Jacqueline Young-De Roover, San Francisco, CA

Savory Zucchini Frittata

This fast and tasty recipe uses up a lot of tasty zucchini! Sometimes I will use a blend of Parmesan, Romano and Gouda cheeses. Serve with a crisp vinaigrette-dressed salad for a lovely brunch.

Makes 8 servings

2 T. olive oil
3 shallots, finely minced
4 cloves garlic, finely minced
6 zucchini, sliced 1/4-inch thick on
 the diagonal
10 eggs, lightly beaten
1/4 t. salt
1/4 t. pepper
1 c. fresh Italian flat-leaf parsley,
 snipped
1/2 c. finely shredded Parmesan
 cheese

Add oil to a large, cast-iron skillet; swirl to coat bottom and sides of pan. Add shallots and garlic; cook over medium heat about one minute. Add zucchini; cook, stirring often, for 5 to 7 minutes, until crisp-tender. Remove pan from heat; add remaining ingredients and mix lightly. Bake in skillet, uncovered, at 325 degrees until set, about 30 minutes. Serve warm or cooled.

Savory Zucchini Frittata

Donna Dye, Ray, OH

Garden-Fresh Denver Omelet

You can add any of your favorite vegetables to this hearty omelet.

Makes 2 servings

2 t. canola oil
2 T. red pepper, diced
2 T. green pepper, diced
2 T. red onion, diced
1 slice turkey bacon, cooked and cut
    into 1/2-inch pieces
2 whole eggs, beaten
3 egg whites
1/4 c. skim milk
1/4 t. pepper
1 t. fresh chives, chopped
Garnish: salsa

Add oil to a cast-iron skillet. Add peppers and onion; cook over low heat, stirring until just wilted, about 5 minutes. Transfer vegetables to a bowl and add bacon. In a separate bowl, beat eggs and egg whites with milk. Season with pepper and whisk in chives. Stir in vegetable mixture. Spray skillet with non-stick vegetable spray. Add half of egg mixture to skillet and cook without stirring, lifting edges to allow uncooked egg to flow underneath. Cover and cook 30 to 45 more seconds, or until eggs are cooked to desired doneness. Gently fold omelet in half; slide onto a plate. Repeat for second omelet. Garnish with salsa.

Nancy Dearborn, Erie, PA

Zucchini Fritters

You'll love these tender pancakes... they're super for a brunch buffet.

Makes 4 servings

1/2 c. all-purpose flour
3/4 t. baking powder
1 T. grated Parmesan cheese
2 eggs, beaten
2 c. zucchini, shredded
2 t. oil for frying
Garnish: plain Greek yogurt,
    chopped fresh parsley

In a medium bowl, combine all ingredients except oil and garnish; stir until mixed. Heat oil in a cast-iron skillet over medium-high heat. Drop batter by 2 tablespoonfuls into skillet. Flatten to 3-inch diameter. Cook and flip until golden on both sides. Serve warm; garnish as desired.

DID YOU KNOW?
Cast iron is great for keeping food warm since it holds heat for a considerable length of time.

Zucchini Fritters

Denise Evans, Moosic, PA

E-Z Home Fries & Eggs

Breakfast cooked in a skillet over a campfire...what a wonderful way to start the day! Speed things up by cooking the potatoes at home to pack in your cooler. Delicious served on toasted English muffins.

Serves 4

2 onions, chopped
1 to 2 t. oil
4 slices bacon, cut into 1-inch pieces
8 potatoes, cooked and diced
4 eggs
pepper, paprika and/or dried parsley
    to taste

In a cast-iron skillet over medium heat, cook onions in oil until tender and golden. Remove onions to a plate and set aside. Add bacon to skillet; cook until crisp. Remove bacon to same plate, reserving drippings in skillet. Add potatoes; cook just until golden. Return onions and bacon to skillet; heat through. Crack eggs over potato mixture. Gently toss mixture until eggs are cooked to desired doneness. Add desired seasonings.

Joshua Logan, Corpus Christi, TX

Egg & Bacon Quesadillas

So quick and so yummy...they will ask for more.

Serves 4

2 T. butter, divided
4 8-inch flour tortillas
5 eggs, beaten
1/2 c. milk
2 8-oz. pkgs. shredded Cheddar
    cheese
6 to 8 slices bacon, crisply cooked
    and crumbled
Optional: salsa, sour cream

Lightly spread about 1/4 teaspoon butter on one side of each tortilla; set aside. In a bowl, beat eggs and milk until combined. Pour egg mixture into a hot, lightly greased cast-iron skillet; cook and stir over medium heat until done. Remove scrambled eggs to a dish and keep warm. Melt remaining butter in the skillet and add a tortilla, buttered-side down. Layer with 1/4 of the cheese, 1/2 of the eggs and 1/2 of the bacon. Top with 1/4 of the cheese and a tortilla, buttered-side up. Cook for one to 2 minutes on each side, until golden. Repeat with remaining ingredients. Cut each into 4 wedges and serve with salsa and sour cream, if desired.

Egg & Bacon Quesadillas

Tamara Ahrens, Sparta, MI

Mom's Everything Waffles

The delicious flavors of peanut butter, pecans and blueberries come together in this one-of-a-kind breakfast favorite.

Makes 10 waffles, serves 10

1-1/4 c. all-purpose flour
1 T. baking powder
1/4 t. salt
2 t. sugar
3/4 c. plus 2 T. quick-cooking oats, uncooked
2 T. wheat germ
3 T. chopped pecans
2 eggs, beaten
2 T. reduced-fat peanut butter
1/2 c. plain Greek yogurt
2-1/2 c. skim milk, divided
3/4 c. fresh blueberries
Garnish: maple syrup, fresh blueberries

Combine flour, baking powder, salt, sugar, oats, wheat germ and nuts in a large bowl; set aside. In a separate bowl, whisk together eggs, peanut butter, yogurt and 2 cups milk. Add to dry ingredients and stir. Add remaining milk as needed to get the consistency of applesauce. Fold in berries. Pour by 1/2 cupfuls onto a preheated cast-iron waffle iron that has been sprayed with non-stick vegetable spray. Bake until crisp, according to manufacturer's directions. Serve with maple syrup and blueberries.

Tina George, El Dorado, AR

Blackberry Skillet Pancake

When I was a little girl, my brothers and I picked blackberries whenever we visited our great-aunt. She had lots of recipes to use up the berries... this is one of them! I have served this for breakfast alongside scrambled eggs & bacon and even as a dessert.

Serves 6

2/3 c. all-purpose flour
1/3 c. sugar
1/4 t. salt
1 c. milk
2 eggs, beaten
1/2 t. vanilla extract
1 t. shortening
2 c. blackberries
3 T. powdered sugar

Combine flour, sugar and salt in a bowl; stir well. Add milk, eggs and vanilla; whisk until smooth. Heat a cast-iron skillet over medium heat until hot and a drop of water sizzles. Brush skillet with shortening. Reduce heat to low; pour batter into skillet. Cover and cook for 10 minutes, until top is firm and puffy and bottom is golden. Top with blackberries and sprinkle with powdered sugar. With a thin spatula, loosen pancake around sides and carefully slide onto a serving dish. Cut into wedges.

Blackberry Skillet Pancake

Gail Blain, Grand Island, NE

Toasted Pecan Pancakes

These very special little pancakes make an ordinary weekend breakfast extraordinary.

Makes about 1-1/2 dozen

2 eggs, beaten
2 T. sugar
1/4 c. butter, melted and cooled
   slightly
1/4 c. maple syrup
1-1/2 c. all-purpose flour
2 t. baking powder
1/2 t. salt
1-1/2 c. milk
2/3 c. chopped toasted pecans
Garnish: additional maple syrup,
   warmed

In a large bowl, whisk together eggs, sugar, butter and syrup. In a separate bowl, mix together flour, baking powder and salt. Add flour mixture and milk alternately to egg mixture, beginning and ending with flour mixture. Stir in pecans. Set a cast-iron skillet over medium heat and brush lightly with oil. Skillet is ready when a few drops of water sizzle when sprinkled on the surface. Pour batter by scant 1/4 cupfuls onto griddle. Cook until bubbles appear on tops and bottoms are golden, about 2 minutes. Turn and cook until golden on the other side, about one minute more. Add a little more oil to griddle for each batch. Serve pancakes with warm maple syrup.

Lois Hobart, Stone Creek, OH

Lemon-Rosemary Breakfast Bread

This zucchini lemon bread is the best! It smells wonderful while it bakes and makes a quick-grab breakfast.

Makes 2 loaves, serves 24

3 c. all-purpose flour
1/2 t. baking powder
2 t. baking soda
2 T. fresh rosemary, minced
2 eggs
1-1/4 c. sugar
1/2 c. butter, melted and slightly
   cooled
1/4 c. olive oil
1 T. lemon zest
3 c. zucchini, grated

In a bowl, whisk together flour, baking powder, baking soda and rosemary; set aside. In a separate large bowl, beat eggs until frothy; beat in sugar, melted butter and olive oil. Stir in lemon zest and zucchini. Add flour mixture to egg mixture; stir until blended. Divide batter into two 9"x4" cast-iron loaf pans sprayed with non-stick vegetable spray. Bake at 350 degrees for 45 to 50 minutes.

Lemon-Rosemary Breakfast Bread

Bev Ray, Brandon, FL

Overnight Buttermilk-Raisin Pancakes

These yummy pancakes are a breakfast time-saver.

Serves 9

2 c. quick-cooking oats, uncooked
2 c. buttermilk
1/2 c. all-purpose flour
2 T. sugar
1 t. baking powder
1 t. baking soda
1/2 t. cinnamon
1/2 t. salt
2 eggs, beaten
1/4 c. butter, melted
1/2 c. raisins
Optional: chopped walnuts
Garnish: syrup

Mix together oats and buttermilk in a medium bowl; cover and refrigerate overnight. Sift together flour, sugar, baking powder, baking soda, cinnamon and salt in a large bowl. Make a well in the center; add oat mixture, eggs, butter and raisins. Stir just until moistened. Allow batter to stand 20 minutes before cooking. If batter is too thick, add buttermilk, one tablespoon at a time, until batter reaches desired consistency. Place a lightly greased, large cast-iron skillet over medium heat. Pour batter by 1/4 cupfuls into skillet. Cook pancakes until bubbles appear on top; flip and cook until golden on both sides. Top with walnuts, if desired, and serve with syrup.

Vickie, Gooseberry Patch

Mini Spinach & Bacon Quiches

These are an elegant addition to a special brunch buffet that can be assembled the night before and refrigerated.

Makes 12 servings

1/4 c. onion, diced
2 t. canola oil
10-oz. pkg. frozen chopped spinach, thawed and drained
1/2 t. pepper
1/8 t. nutmeg
2 slices bacon, crisply cooked and crumbled
15-oz. container low-fat ricotta cheese
8-oz. pkg. shredded part-skim mozzarella cheese
1/4 c. grated Parmesan cheese
3 eggs, beaten

In a cast-iron skillet over medium heat, cook onion in oil until tender. Add spinach and seasonings; stir over medium heat about 3 minutes or until liquid evaporates. Remove from heat; stir in bacon and cool. Combine cheeses in a large bowl. Add eggs; stir until well blended. Add cooled spinach mixture; stir until well blended. Divide mixture evenly among 12 lightly greased muffin cups. Bake at 350 degrees for 40 minutes or until filling is set. Let stand 10 minutes; run a thin knife around edges to release. Serve warm.

Mini Spinach & Bacon Quiches

Cindy Whitney, Bar Mills, ME

Apple-Cinnamon Pancakes

Serve this beautiful breakfast anytime!

Makes 6 servings

1 c. whole-wheat flour
1 T. sugar
1 t. baking powder
1/4 t. baking soda
1 t. cinnamon
1 c. buttermilk
1 egg, beaten
2 T. oil
1 McIntosh apple, quartered, cored
    and grated
Garnish: raspberry sauce, plain Greek
    yogurt, fresh raspberries

Sift together dry ingredients; set aside. Whisk together buttermilk, egg and oil; add to dry ingredients. Stir batter until smooth; don't overbeat. Pour batter by 1/4 cupfuls onto a lightly greased hot cast-iron griddle. Cook until bubbles appear on the surface. Sprinkle with 2 teaspoons apple; turn and continue cooking for an additional 2 to 3 minutes, until golden. Serve warm. Garnish as desired.

Jill Ross, Pickerington, OH

Breezy Brunch Skillet

Try this all-in-one breakfast on your next camp-out! Just set the skillet on a grate over hot coals.

Serves 4 to 6

6 slices bacon, diced
6 c. frozen diced potatoes
3/4 c. green pepper, chopped
1/2 c. onion, chopped
1 t. salt
1/4 t. pepper
4 to 6 eggs
1/2 c. shredded Cheddar cheese

In a large cast-iron skillet over medium-high heat, cook bacon until crisp. Drain and set aside, reserving 2 tablespoons drippings in skillet. Add potatoes, green pepper, onion, salt and pepper to drippings. Cook and stir for 2 minutes. Cover and cook for about 15 minutes, stirring occasionally, until potatoes are golden and tender. With a spoon, make 4 to 6 wells in potato mixture. Crack one egg into each well, taking care not to break the yolks. Cover and cook over low heat for 8 to 10 minutes, until eggs are completely set. Sprinkle with cheese and crumbled bacon.

Breezy Brunch Skillet

Judy Mitchell, Huntley, IL

Judy's Famous Banana Muffins

Our local newspaper featured me as "Cook of the Week" with this recipe! I found the original recipe many years ago and have revised it over the years. It's a favorite of family & friends.

Makes one dozen, serves 12

3 very ripe bananas, mashed
2 eggs, beaten
1/2 c. canola oil
1/2 c. plus 1 T. sugar, divided
1/2 c. quick-cooking oats, uncooked
1/2 c. whole-wheat flour
1/2 c. all-purpose flour
1/2 c. wheat germ
1 t. vanilla extract
1 t. baking powder
1/2 t. baking soda
1/4 t. salt
1/4 c. chopped walnuts

In a large bowl, stir together bananas, eggs, oil and 1/2 cup sugar until combined. Add remaining ingredients except walnuts and remaining sugar; stir just until blended. Spoon batter into greased cast-iron muffin cups, filling 2/3 full. Sprinkle tops with walnuts and remaining sugar. Bake at 350 degrees for 20 to 25 minutes, until golden and a toothpick tests clean. Let muffins cool in pan for 5 minutes; remove to a wire rack and cool completely.

Tammy Burnett, Springfield, MO

Dutch Oven Campers' Breakfast

When we go camping, we often have a big group of 20 to 25 family members. This breakfast feeds lots of us! Add whatever veggies you like... these are ones we always seem to have on hand. Yum!

Serves 12 to 15

1 lb. bacon, chopped
2 green and/or red peppers, diced
2 c. onion, diced
12 potatoes, sliced or diced
salt and pepper to taste
1 doz. eggs
1/4 c. water
2 c. shredded Cheddar cheese

In a campfire ring, set a Dutch oven over 15 to 18 hot briquettes until heated. Add bacon; cook until crisp and golden. Add peppers and onion; cook until onion is translucent. Push half of the briquettes to one side; set Dutch oven on remaining briquets. Add potatoes; season with salt and pepper. Cover Dutch oven with lid; place about 14 briquets on top of lid. Cook for 30 minutes, or until potatoes are tender. Whisk together eggs and water; pour over potatoes. Cover, adding more hot briquettes to lid as needed. Cook another 15 to 20 minutes, stirring every 5 minutes, until eggs are set. Top with cheese; cover and let stand until cheese is melted.

Dutch Oven Campers' Breakfast

Sonya Labbe, Quebec, Canada

Hashbrown Quiche

A hearty quiche baked in a crust of hashbrowns! Enjoy it for breakfast, or add a zesty salad and have breakfast for dinner.

Serves 4 to 6

3 c. frozen shredded hashbrowns, thawed
1/4 c. butter, melted
3 eggs, beaten
1 c. half-and-half
3/4 c. cooked ham, diced
1/2 c. green onions, chopped
1 c. shredded Cheddar cheese
salt and pepper to taste

In a cast-iron skillet, combine hashbrowns and butter. Press into the bottom and up the sides of skillet. Transfer the skillet to oven. Bake, uncovered, at 450 degrees for 20 to 25 minutes, until crisp and golden. Remove from oven; cool slightly. Combine remaining ingredients in a bowl; pour mixture over the hashbrowns. Reduce the oven temperature to 350 degrees. Bake for another 30 minutes, or until quiche is golden and set.

Renae Scheiderer, Beallsville, OH

Festive Brunch Frittata

Serve this delicious egg dish in the skillet that you cook it in for a fun and rustic look.

Serves 6

8 eggs, beaten
1/2 t. salt
1/8 t. pepper
1/2 c. shredded Cheddar cheese
2 T. butter
2 c. red, green and yellow peppers, chopped
1/4 c. onion, chopped
Garnish: chopped fresh parsley

Beat together eggs, salt and pepper. Fold in Cheddar cheese and set aside. Melt butter over medium heat in a cast-iron skillet. Add peppers and onion to skillet; sauté until tender. Pour eggs over peppers and onion; don't stir. Cover and cook over low heat for about 9 minutes. Eggs are set when frittata is lightly golden on the underside. Turn oven on broil. Move skillet from stovetop to oven; broil top about 5 inches from heat until lightly golden. Garnish with parsley.

FLAVOR BOOST
Add your favorite meat such as crisp bacon, cooked sausage or chopped pepperoni for a hearty change of pace.

Festive Brunch Frittata

Lisa Sanders, Shoals, IN

Garden Bounty Egg Bake

I came up with this easy recipe to help my husband Jim enjoy eating more vegetables. He loves eggs, so what better way to get him to eat veggies! You can have the veggies cut up the night before so prep time is a snap.

Makes 8 servings

10 eggs
1/2 c. skim milk
1 T. dried parsley
1 t. dried thyme
1 t. garlic powder
1/8 t. salt
1/8 t. pepper
1 T. olive oil
8-oz. pkg. sliced mushrooms
1/2 c. onion, diced
1/2 c. green pepper, diced
1/2 c. carrot, peeled and shredded
1/2 c. broccoli, chopped
1/2 c. tomato, chopped
3/4 c. shredded Cheddar cheese
Optional: hot pepper sauce

In a bowl, whisk together eggs and milk; stir in seasonings and set aside. Heat oil in a large cast-iron skillet over medium-high heat. Add all vegetables except tomato; sauté until crisp-tender. Add tomato to skillet. Pour egg mixture over vegetable mixture; remove skillet to the oven. Bake at 350 degrees for about 15 to 20 minutes, until a knife tip inserted in the center tests clean. Sprinkle with cheese; return to oven until cheese melts. Serve with hot pepper sauce, if desired.

Linda Bonwill, Englewood, FL

Spinach & Tomato French Toast

A healthier way to make French toast...plus, it looks so pretty! We like to use thinly sliced whole-grain toast but brioche bread toast is great too.

Serves 4

3 eggs
salt and pepper to taste
8 slices whole grain bread
4 c. fresh spinach, torn
2 tomatoes, sliced
shaved Parmesan cheese

In a bowl, beat eggs with salt and pepper. Dip bread slices into egg. Place in a lightly greased cast-iron skillet over medium heat; cook one side until lightly golden. Place fresh spinach, tomato slice and cheese onto each slice, pressing lightly to secure. Flip and briefly cook on other side until cooked. Flip over and serve open-face.

FLAVOR BOOST
Add crisply-cooked bacon to this open-faced sandwich for a meatier version of this dish.

Spinach & Tomato French Toast

Jackie Smulski, Lyons, IL

Scrambled Eggs & Lox

These eggs are sure to please everyone. We love them with toasted English muffins.

Serves 6

6 eggs, beaten
1 T. fresh dill, minced
1 T. fresh chives, minced
1 T. green onion, minced
pepper to taste
2 T. butter
4-oz. pkg. smoked salmon, diced

Whisk together eggs, herbs, onion and pepper. Melt butter in a large cast-iron skillet over medium heat. Add egg mixture and stir gently with a fork or spatula until eggs begin to set. Stir in salmon and continue cooking eggs to desired doneness.

Melody Taynor, Everett, WA

Sunrise Skillet

When our kids want to camp out in the backyard, I just have to wake them to the aroma of a delicious breakfast...and this recipe does the trick every time.

Serves 6 to 8

1/2 lb. bacon
4 c. potatoes, peeled and cubed
1/2 onion, chopped
6 eggs, beaten
1 c. shredded Cheddar cheese
Optional: chopped green onions

Cook bacon in a cast-iron skillet over the slow-burning coals of a campfire or on a stove over medium heat until crisply cooked. Remove bacon from skillet; set aside. Stir potatoes and onion into drippings. Cover and cook until potatoes are tender, about 10 to 12 minutes. Crumble bacon into potatoes. Stir in eggs; cover and cook until set, about 2 minutes. Sprinkle with cheese; let stand until the cheese melts. Garnish with green onions, if desired.

Sunrise Skillet

Paula Zsiray, Logan, UT

Hashbrown Skillet Omelet

Set out the catsup and hot pepper sauce...everyone can spice up their portion as they like.

Serves 6

1/2 lb. bacon
2 T. oil
3 c. frozen shredded hashbrowns
1-1/2 c. shredded Cheddar or
    Cheddar Jack cheese, divided
6 eggs, beaten
1/4 c. water
1 T. fresh parsley, chopped
1/2 t. paprika

Cook bacon in a cast-iron skillet over medium-high heat until crisp. Remove bacon to paper towels. Drain skillet; add oil to skillet. Add frozen hashbrowns and cook without turning for about 10 minutes, until golden. Turn carefully; cook other side until golden. Remove skillet from heat. Sprinkle hashbrowns with crumbled bacon and one cup shredded cheese. Beat eggs and water; pour over cheese. Sprinkle with parsley and paprika. Transfer skillet to oven. Bake, uncovered, at 350 degrees for 20 to 25 minutes, until eggs are set in the center. Remove from oven; sprinkle with remaining cheese and let stand for 5 minutes. Cut into wedges.

Julie Ann Perkins, Anderson, IN

Peanut Butter French Toast

Who can resist the classic taste of peanut butter & jelly? Make it for breakfast for a real treat.

Serves 2

4 slices white or whole-wheat bread
1/2 c. creamy peanut butter
2 T. grape jelly
3 eggs, beaten
1/4 c. milk
2 T. butter
Garnish: powdered sugar

Use bread, peanut butter and jelly to make 2 sandwiches; set aside. In a bowl, whisk together eggs and milk. Dip each sandwich into egg mixture. Melt butter in a cast-iron skillet over medium heat. Add sandwiches to skillet and cook until golden, about 2 to 3 minutes on each side. Sprinkle with powdered sugar; cut diagonally into triangles.

Peanut Butter French Toast

Garbanzo Bean Soup, p. 110

CHAPTER TWO

SATISFYING
Soups & Sandwiches

Zesty Minestrone, p. 68

Carol's Veggie Panini, p. 94

Kendall Hale, Lynn, MA

Cheese & Garlic Croutons

These savory croutons are delicious sprinkled in a bowl of soup or tossed in a dinner salad.

Makes 2 cups

1/2 c. butter
1/2 t. dried oregano
1/2 t. dried basil
1/2 t. celery salt
2 cloves garlic, minced
1 T. onion, minced
2 c. whole-wheat bread, cubed
2 T. grated Parmesan cheese

Melt butter in a large cast-iron skillet. Add seasonings, garlic and onion; cook for about one minute to soften. Stir in bread cubes; sauté until golden and crisp. Toss with cheese until coated. Cool; store in an airtight container.

Nancy Campbell, Bellingham, WA

Veggie Patch Stew

A family favorite, made with fresh veggies from our summer garden.

Makes 6 servings

3 zucchini, sliced
3 yellow squash, sliced
2 onions, chopped
2 tomatoes, chopped
1 eggplant, peeled and cubed
1 green pepper, chopped
1 clove garlic, minced
2 T. butter, softened
1 t. hot pepper sauce
1/2 t. curry powder
1 t. chili powder
salt and pepper to taste
Garnish: shredded mozzarella
   cheese

Place all vegetables in a large Dutch oven over low heat. Stir in remaining ingredients except cheese. Cover and simmer for one hour, stirring frequently. Do not add any liquid, as vegetables make their own juice. Top portions with cheese before serving.

Veggie Patch Stew

Patty Flak, Erie, PA

Reuben Sandwich

Everyone's favorite deli sandwich!

Makes one sandwich

3 slices deli corned beef
1 to 2 slices Swiss cheese
2 slices pumpernickel or dark rye
  bread
1/4 c. sauerkraut, well drained
1-1/2 T. Thousand Island salad
  dressing
3 T. butter

Arrange corned beef and cheese on one slice of bread. Heap with sauerkraut; drizzle with salad dressing. Add second bread slice. Melt butter in a cast-iron skillet over medium heat. Add sandwich; grill on both sides until golden and cheese melts.

Amy Butcher, Columbus, GA

Dijon Beef Stew

A loaf of crusty French bread, a salad of mixed greens and steamy bowls of this stew...what could be better?

Makes 6 to 8 servings

1-1/2 lbs. stew beef cubes
1/4 c. all-purpose flour
2 T. oil
salt and pepper to taste
2 14-1/2 oz. cans diced tomatoes
    with garlic and onion
14-1/2 oz. can beef broth
4 carrots, peeled and sliced
2 potatoes, peeled and cubed
3/4 t. dried thyme
2 T. Dijon mustard

Combine beef and flour in a large plastic zipping bag; toss to coat evenly. Add oil to a cast-iron Dutch oven over medium-high heat. Brown beef; season with salt and pepper. Drain; add tomatoes with juice and remaining ingredients except mustard. Bring to a boil; reduce heat to medium-low. Cover and simmer for one hour, or until beef is tender. Stir in mustard.

Dijon Beef Stew

Lisa Johnson, Hallsville, TX

Lisa's Chicken Tortilla Soup

My family loves this on a cold winter night.

Makes 8 servings

4 14-1/2 oz. cans low-sodium
    chicken broth
4 10-oz. cans diced tomatoes with
    green chiles
1 c. canned or frozen corn
30-oz. can refried beans
4-3/4 c. cooked chicken, shredded
Garnish: shredded Mexican-blend
    cheese, corn chips or tortilla
    strips, chopped fresh cilantro

Combine broth and tomatoes with chiles in a Dutch oven over medium heat. Stir in corn and beans; bring to a boil. Reduce heat to low and simmer 5 minutes, stirring frequently. Add chicken and heat through. Garnish bowls of soup as desired.

Diane Axtell, Marble Falls, TX

Easy Salsa Chili

This chili is quick & easy to make because it's served from the same skillet it's made in! Salsa gives it lots of zip and melting the cheese in the chili just before serving makes it rich and yummy.

Serves 6

1 lb. ground beef
1 T. fresh parsley, chopped
1 T. fresh chives, chopped
1 T. fresh basil, chopped
28-oz. can crushed tomatoes
14-1/2 oz. can fire-roasted diced
    tomatoes
3/4 c. chunky salsa
3/4 c. water
14-1/2 oz. can black beans
1 t. chili powder
1 t. red pepper flakes
1 t. salt
1 t. pepper
1/2 c. shredded Cheddar cheese
Garnish: additional cheese, chopped
    avocado, chopped fresh chives,
    fresh cilantro

Brown beef in a cast-iron skillet over medium heat; drain. Add parsley, chives and basil; cook another minute, or until herbs are just cooked. Add tomatoes with juice, salsa, water, beans and seasonings. Reduce heat to medium-low. Simmer for 20 minutes, stirring occasionally. Add cheese just before serving. Ladle into bowls; garnish as desired. Serve immediately.

Easy Salsa Chili

Dawn Henning, Hillard, Ohio

Greek Chicken & Rice Soup

When you serve a rotisserie chicken with rice for supper, reserve some to enjoy in soup for the next night.

Makes 6 servings

4 c. low-sodium chicken broth
2 c. cooked white rice, divided
2 egg yolks, beaten
1 T. lemon zest
3 T. lemon juice
1-1/2 c. cooked chicken, shredded
1/4 t. salt
1/2 t. pepper
Garnish: sliced black olives, lemon slices, fresh dill or parsley, chopped

Bring broth to a simmer in a Dutch oven over medium heat. Transfer one cup hot broth to a blender. Add 1/2 cup cooked rice, egg yolks, lemon zest and juice to blender; cover and blend until smooth. Stir rice mixture into simmering broth; add chicken and remaining rice. Simmer, stirring frequently, about 10 minutes, until slightly thickened. Add salt and pepper to taste. Garnish as desired.

Meg Dickinson, Champaign, IL

Black Bean Breakfast Burritos

My husband and I love the idea of eating breakfast for dinner so I tried this combination, and it was yummy!

Makes 6 burritos, serves 6

2 T. olive oil
1/2 c. onion, chopped
1/2 c. green pepper, chopped
3 cloves garlic, minced
16-oz. can black beans, drained and rinsed
10-oz. can diced tomatoes with green chiles
1 t. fajita seasoning mix
6 eggs, beaten
1/2 c. green onion, chopped
1 T. Fiesta Dip Mix
6 8-inch flour tortillas, warmed
1/2 c. shredded Cheddar cheese

Heat oil in a Dutch oven over medium heat. Add onion, green pepper and garlic; sauté until tender. Stir in beans, tomatoes and fajita seasoning. Bring to a simmer and let cook about 10 minutes. Meanwhile, in a bowl, whisk together eggs, green onion and one tablespoon Fiesta Dip Mix. Scramble egg mixture in a lightly greased skillet. To serve, top each tortilla with a spoonful of bean mixture, a spoonful of scrambled eggs and a sprinkle of cheese; roll up tortilla.

Fiesta Dip Mix:
2 T. dried parsley
4 t. dried, minced onion
4 t. chili powder
1 T. dried cumin
1 T. dried chives
1 t. salt

Mix all ingredients well; store in a small jar. Makes about 1/2 cup.

Black Bean Breakfast Burritos

Becky Hall, Belton, MO

Kitchen Cabinet Mild White Chili

This recipe was created on a cold night with ingredients from the kitchen cabinet. It can easily be spiced up with a can of diced chiles or chopped jalapeño peppers.

Makes 4 servings

2 15-1/2 oz. cans Great Northern
    beans
Optional: 4-1/2 oz. can diced
    green chiles
14-oz. can chicken broth
1 T. dried, minced onion
1 T. red pepper flakes
1-1/2 t. dried, minced garlic
1 t. ground cumin
1/2 t. dried oregano
1/8 t. cayenne pepper
1/8t. ground cloves
1-1/2 c. cooked chicken, chopped
4-oz. can sliced mushrooms, drained
Garnish: 1 c. shredded sharp
    Cheddar cheese

In a Dutch oven, combine all ingredients except chicken, mushrooms and cheese. Cook over medium heat for 5 minutes; bring to a boil. Reduce heat and simmer 5 minutes. Add chicken and mushrooms; simmer, uncovered, for 8 to 10 minutes, until heated through. Serve with cheese.

Kimberly Ascroft, Merritt Island, FL.

Key West Burgers

Dress up a plain burger with a tropical touch using slices of mango and fresh lime juice.

Makes 4 servings

1 lb. lean ground beef
3 T. Key lime juice
1/4 c. fresh cilantro, chopped,
    divided
salt and pepper to taste
4 whole-wheat hamburger buns,
    split and toasted
1 mango, pitted, peeled and sliced
Garnish: lettuce

In a bowl, combine beef, lime juice, 3 tablespoons cilantro, salt and pepper. Form beef mixture into 4 patties. Spray a large cast-iron skillet with non-stick vegetable spray. Cook patties over medium heat for 6 minutes. Flip patties, cover skillet and cook for another 6 minutes. Place lettuce on bottom halves of buns and top with patties. Add Creamy Burger Spread onto bun tops. Top with mango slices and remaining chopped cilantro. Add bun tops.

Creamy Burger Spread:
1/2 c. light cream cheese, softened
1/2 c. plain Greek yogurt
3 green onion tops, chopped

Combine all ingredients until completely blended. Cover and refrigerate at least 15 minutes.

Key West Burgers

Jo Ann, Gooseberry Patch

Dressed Oyster Po'boys

These sandwiches are piled high with plump fried oysters and slaw...all atop a tangy sauce. Mmm...it's good!

Serves 4

1-1/2 c. self-rising cornmeal
1-1/2 T. salt-free Cajun seasoning, divided
2 12-oz. containers fresh shucked oysters, drained
peanut or vegetable oil for frying
1 c. mayonnaise, divided
2 T. Dijon mustard
2 T. white vinegar
6 c. finely shredded multicolored cabbage
2 T. catsup
1 T. prepared horseradish
3/4 t. paprika
4 hoagie rolls, split and toasted

Combine cornmeal and one tablespoon Cajun seasoning; dredge oysters in mixture. Pour oil into a Dutch oven to a depth of 2 inches and put on medium heat. Heat to 375 degrees. Fry oysters, in 3 batches, 2 to 3 minutes or until golden. Drain on wire racks. Stir together 1/2 cup mayonnaise, mustard and vinegar. Stir in cabbage; set slaw aside. Stir together remaining mayonnaise, catsup, horseradish, Cajun seasoning and paprika. Spread bottom halves of rolls with mayonnaise mixture. Layer with oysters and top with slaw; cover with roll tops.

Tanya Graham, Lawrenceville, GA

Chili with Corn Dumplings

Dumplings created with cornmeal and fresh cilantro make this chili extra special and so satisfying.

Serves 10

4-1/2 lbs. ground beef
2-1/2 c. chopped onion
3 15-oz. cans corn, divided
3 14-1/2 oz. cans stewed tomatoes
3 15-oz. cans tomato sauce
1 T. hot pepper sauce
6 T. chili powder
1 T. garlic, minced
1-1/3 c. biscuit baking mix
2/3 c. cornmeal
2/3 c. milk
3 T. fresh cilantro, chopped

Brown ground beef and onion in a Dutch oven over medium heat; drain. Set aside 1-1/2 cups corn; stir remaining corn with liquid, tomatoes with liquid, sauces, chili powder and garlic into beef mixture. Bring to a boil. Reduce heat; cover and simmer 15 minutes. Combine baking mix and cornmeal in a medium bowl; stir in milk, cilantro and reserved corn just until moistened. Drop dough by rounded tablespoonfuls onto simmering chili. Cook over low heat, uncovered, 15 minutes. Cover and cook 15 to 18 more minutes or until dumplings are dry on top.

Chili with Corn Dumplings

Janet Parsons, Pickerington, OH

Bean & Sausage Soup

If you like pasta, cook ditalini or elbows separately and add 1/2 cup to each serving.

Serves 6

5 Italian pork sausage links
1/4 c. onion, diced
3 cloves garlic, minced
1 t. olive oil
1 t. salt
1/4 t. red pepper flakes
15-oz. can diced tomatoes
32-oz. container chicken broth
2 15-oz. cans white kidney beans
4 c. spinach, torn
Garnish: grated Parmesan cheese

In a Dutch oven, sauté sausage, onion and garlic in oil until sausage is golden. Remove sausage links and slice into one-inch pieces; return to pot. Add remaining ingredients except garnish. Cover and bring to a boil. Reduce heat to low; simmer, covered, for 2 to3 hours, stirring occasionally. Garnish with cheese.

DID YOU KNOW
The more you use your cast-iron pans, the smoother the surface of the pans becomes. That is why old cast-iron cookware is so special to use.

Lydia Edgy, Patterson, MO

Chicken, White Bean & Pasta Soup

Such a pretty soup! We love the chunks of chicken combined with the pasta and fresh spinach.

Makes 10 servings

1 onion, chopped
4 carrots, peeled and sliced
4 stalks celery, sliced
2 T. olive oil
4 c. low-sodium chicken broth
3 c. water, divided
2 boneless, skinless chicken breasts, cooked and diced
2 15-1/2 oz. cans Great Northern beans, drained
6 cherry tomatoes, diced
1/2 t. dried thyme
1/2 t. dried rosemary
1/4 t. salt
1/4 t. pepper
1 c. rotini pasta, uncooked
1/2 lb. baby spinach

In a Dutch oven over medium heat, sauté onion, carrots and celery in oil. Add broth and 2 cups water. Bring to a boil; simmer for 10 minutes. Stir in chicken, beans, tomatoes and seasonings. Reduce heat to low; cover and simmer for 25 to 30 minutes. Return to a boil; stir in pasta. Cook until pasta is tender, about 10 minutes. Add remaining water if soup is too thick. Stir in spinach and cook for 2 minutes, or until wilted.

Chicken, White Bean & Pasta Soup

Jo Ann, Gooseberry Patch

Farmstead Split Pea Soup

Fill a thermos with this hearty soup... it's terrific for an autumn picnic.

Serves 6

8 c. water
16-oz. pkg. split peas, rinsed and
    drained
1-1/2 lb. ham bone with meat
2 onions, chopped
3 leeks, white part only, chopped
2 stalks celery, chopped
1 carrot, peeled and chopped
1 c. dry white wine or vegetable
    broth
1 clove garlic, finely chopped
1/2 t. dried marjoram
1/4 t. dried thyme
salt and pepper to taste

Combine all ingredients except salt and pepper in a Dutch oven. Bring to a boil. Cover, reduce heat and simmer for 2 to 2-1/2 hours, stirring occasionally, until peas are soft. Remove ham bone and cool to warm. Remove meat from bone and add to Dutch oven. Add salt and pepper to taste.

Beth Parrish, Linn, MO

Best-Ever Grilled Cheese Sandwiches

We love this rich, cheesy spread on thick slices of bakery-fresh sourdough or Italian bread.

Makes 4 to 5 sandwiches

3-oz. pkg. cream cheese, softened
3/4 c. mayonnaise-type salad
    dressing
1 c. shredded mozzarella cheese
1 c. shredded Cheddar cheese
1/4 t. garlic powder
1/8 t. seasoned salt
8 to 10 slices white bread
2 T. butter, softened

Blend cream cheese and salad dressing until smooth; stir in cheeses, garlic powder and salt. Spread half the bread slices with cheese mixture. Top with remaining bread; spread butter on both sides of sandwiches. Grill in a cast-iron skillet over medium heat until golden on both sides.

Best-Ever Grilled Cheese Sandwiches

Kristin Stone, Little Elm, TX

Kristin's Peasant Stew

I call this Peasant Stew because it's so easy on the budget! It is also easy to make and everyone always loves it. I serve it with warm whole-grain bread and Cheddar cheese. Yum!

Makes 6 servings

1 eggplant, peeled and thickly sliced
1/4 t. salt
2 T. olive oil
2 zucchini, halved lengthwise and thickly sliced
2 t. dried basil
1/8 t. garlic salt
4 c. chicken broth
1/2 c. elbow macaroni, uncooked
15-oz. can kidney beans, drained and rinsed

Sprinkle eggplant slices with salt on both sides. Let stand for 30 minutes; rinse well, drain and chop. Heat oil in a Dutch oven over medium heat. Add eggplant, zucchini and seasonings; sauté until vegetables are crisp-tender. Add broth; bring to a boil. Stir in macaroni. Reduce heat and simmer for 10 minutes, or until macaroni is tender. Stir in beans; heat through.

Beth Hagopian, Huntsville, AL

Zesty Minestrone

This delicious soup reheats well...a great make-ahead for tailgate parties!

Makes 6 to 8 servings

1 lb. Italian pork sausage links, sliced
2 t. oil
1 onion, chopped
1 green pepper, chopped
3 cloves garlic, chopped
28-oz. can whole tomatoes
2 potatoes, peeled and diced
1/4 c. fresh parsley, chopped
2 t. dried oregano
1 t. dried basil
1 t. fennel seed
1/2 t. red pepper flakes
salt and pepper to taste
4 c. beef broth
2 16-oz. cans kidney beans
1 c. elbow macaroni, uncooked

Sauté sausage in oil in a Dutch oven over medium heat; drain. Add onion, green pepper and garlic; cook for 5 minutes. Add tomatoes with juice, potatoes, seasonings and beef broth; bring to a boil. Reduce heat; simmer for 30 minutes. Stir in undrained beans and uncooked macaroni. Simmer an additional 10 minutes, or until macaroni is tender.

Zesty Minestrone

Sandy Coffey, Cincinnati, OH

Mom's German Potato Soup

We love to try different soups in fall and winter. This one is a big favorite. Grab a cup and sit by the fire with us!

Makes 6 servings

2 T. butter
2 onions, chopped
2 cloves garlic, minced
3 stalks celery, thinly sliced
3 potatoes, diced
2 14-oz. cans chicken broth
1-1/2 c. milk
salt and pepper to taste
1 c. shredded Longhorn cheese

Melt butter in a Dutch oven over medium-high heat. Sauté onions, garlic and celery for 3 to 5 minutes. Add potatoes and chicken broth. Simmer, uncovered, for about 30 minutes, stirring often, until vegetables are very tender. Remove soup from heat. Add soup to a blender, 1/3 at a time, and process until smooth. (Or mash with a potato masher.) Return soup to Dutch oven. Stir in milk; season with salt and pepper. Reheat but do not boil. Serve individual bowls sprinkled with cheese.

Irene Whatling, West Des Moines, IA

Peanut Butter Apple-Bacon Sandwich

My family loves this grilled sandwich. I make it for lunch once a week! Sometimes I add some mild Cheddar cheese instead of the peanut butter.

Makes 4 sandwiches

8 slices applewood smoked bacon
8 slices whole-grain bread
1/4 c. peach preserves
1 to 2 apples, cored and thinly sliced
1/4 c. creamy peanut butter
2 to 3 T. butter, softened and divided

In a cast-iron skillet over medium heat, cook bacon until crisp; drain bacon on paper towels. Spread 4 slices of bread with preserves; layer apple and bacon slices over preserves. Spread remaining bread slices with peanut butter; close sandwiches. Spread tops of sandwiches with half of butter. Place sandwiches butter-side down on a griddle over medium heat. Spread remaining butter on unbuttered side of sandwiches. Cook 2 to 3 minutes per side, until bread is toasted and sandwiches are heated through. Serve warm.

Peanut Butter Apple-Bacon Sandwich

Laura Fuller, Fort Wayne, IN

Caroline's Leek Soup

If you have never tried leeks, this is a good recipe to start with. They are milder than onions but have so much flavor! They pair so well with the cauliflower in this soup.

Makes 4 servings

1 leek, halved lengthwise and sliced
1 t. butter
1 T. water
1 head cauliflower, cut into 1-inch
    pieces
3/4 t. coriander
14-1/2 oz. can low-sodium chicken
    broth
1-1/4 c. milk
1/4 t. salt
1/4 t. pepper
Garnish: 1 T. sliced almonds

Rinse leek well in cold water; pat dry. In a Dutch oven over medium-high heat, combine butter and water. Add leek and cauliflower; cook for 5 minutes. Stir in remaining ingredients except garnish and bring to a boil. Reduce heat to low and simmer, covered, 20 minutes. Transfer soup in batches to a blender; purée until smooth. Garnish servings with almonds.

Lizzy Burnley, Ankeny, IA

Easy Sloppy Joes

Instant brown rice makes this Sloppy Joe easy to make and a little bit healthier.

Serves 6

1-1/2 lbs. ground beef
1 T. beef bouillon granules
1/2 c. instant brown rice, uncooked
1/4 c. catsup
1/2 c. water
salt and pepper to taste
6 hamburger buns, split

Brown beef in a cast-iron skillet until all the pink in beef is gone. Drain and return to skillet. Add remaining ingredients except buns and bring to a boil. Boil for one minute. Remove from heat and cover for 10 minutes. Serve on hamburger buns.

FLAVOR BOOST
Add 2 tablespoons of chopped red pepper to the meat mixture for extra flavor and color.

Easy Sloppy Joes

Elena Nelson, Concordia, MO

So-Easy Pork Fritters

This is my husband's favorite meal. I created this recipe to mimic a menu item at our favorite restaurant. These fritters are excellent in a sandwich too.

Serves 4

1 lb. pork tenderloin, sliced 1/2-inch thick
1 egg, beaten
3 T. milk
1 sleeve saltine crackers, finely crushed
3/4 c. all-purpose flour
1 t. salt
1/2 t. pepper
oil for frying

Flatten pork with a meat mallet; set aside. Place egg and milk in a small bowl and blend well. Combine cracker crumbs, flour and seasonings in a separate bowl. Dip pork slices into egg mixture, then press in crumb mixture until well coated. Heat 1/2 inch of oil in a cast-iron skillet over medium-high heat. Add pork slices; fry until deep golden on both sides and no longer pink in the middle, turning as needed.

Judy Voster, Neenah, WI

Corn & Bacon Chowder

The contrast of sweet corn and smoky bacon makes this delicious comfort food. For added texture, stir in 1/2 cup frozen corn kernels and then sprinkle with an extra slice of crisp, chopped bacon to finish.

Serves 8

8 slices bacon, diced
1 c. onion, chopped
3 14-1/2 oz. cans chicken broth
2 c. whole milk
4 c. potatoes, peeled and diced
4 c. fresh or frozen corn
salt and pepper to taste
Garnish: chopped fresh chives

Cook bacon in a Dutch oven over medium heat until almost crisp; drain excess fat, reserving one tablespoon of drippings. Add onion and cook until tender. Add broth, milk, potatoes and corn; cover and bring to a boil. Reduce heat; simmer 12 to 15 minutes, until potatoes are tender. Add salt and pepper to taste; garnish with parsley.

Corn & Bacon Chowder

Angie Venable, Ostrander, OH

Open-Faced Lone Star Burgers

I first saw a chicken version of this recipe on the cover of a magazine. I decided to make it with burgers instead. Yum!

Makes 6 servings

1/4 c. onion, chopped
2 cloves garlic, minced
1/4 t. dried thyme
1-1/2 c. shredded Colby Jack cheese, divided
1-1/2 lbs. ground beef
6 slices frozen garlic Texas toast
8-oz. can tomato sauce
1 T. brown sugar, packed
1 t. Worcestershire sauce
1 t. steak sauce

In a large bowl, combine onion, garlic, thyme and one cup cheese. Crumble beef over top and mix well. Form into 6 oval-shaped patties. In a large cast-iron skillet, cook patties over medium heat for 5 to 6 minutes per side, to desired doneness. Meanwhile, prepare toast according to package directions. Drain patties; set aside and keep warm. Add remaining ingredients to the skillet. Bring to a boil; cook and stir for 2 minutes, or until slightly thickened. Return burgers to skillet; turn to coat. Sprinkle with remaining cheese. Serve burgers on toast.

Linda Marshall, Ontario, Canada

Black Beans & Vegetable Chili

This vegetarian chili, filled with black beans, peppers, squash and tomatoes, is hearty and filling.

Serves 4 to 6

1 onion, coarsely chopped
1 T. oil
28-oz. can diced tomatoes
2/3 c. picante sauce
1-1/2 t. ground cumin
1 t. salt
1/2 t. dried basil
15-oz. can black beans, drained and rinsed
1 green pepper, cut into 3/4-inch pieces
1 red pepper, cut into 3/4-inch pieces
1 yellow squash or zucchini, cut into 1/2-inch pieces
hot cooked rice
Garnish: shredded Cheddar cheese, sour cream, chopped fresh cilantro
Optional: additional picante sauce

Sauté onion in oil in a Dutch oven over medium-high heat, stirring constantly, until tender. Add tomatoes with juice, picante sauce and seasonings; stir well. Bring to a boil; cover, reduce heat and simmer 5 minutes. Stir in beans, peppers and squash. Cover and cook over medium-low heat 25 minutes or until vegetables are tender, stirring occasionally. To serve, ladle chili over hot cooked rice in individual bowls. Top each serving with cheese, sour cream and cilantro. Serve with additional picante sauce, if desired.

Black Beans & Vegetable Chili

Vickie, Gooseberry Patch

Basil & Tomato Soup

Fresh basil is unsurpassed in summer dishes...it adds a spicy, flavorful goodness that can't be beat. Try it in this garden-fresh soup.

Serves 6 to 8

2 T. oil
1 onion, chopped
2 to 3 tomatoes, chopped
1-1/2 lbs. yellow squash, chopped
3 c. chicken broth
1 c. buttermilk
1/4 c. fresh basil, minced
Garnish: fresh basil sprigs

Heat oil in a cast-iron skillet over medium heat. Sauté onion until tender, about 5 minutes. Add tomatoes and continue to cook for 5 minutes, or until tomatoes are soft. Stir in squash and chicken broth; bring to a boil. Reduce heat and simmer 15 minutes, or until squash is fork-tender. Working in batches, spoon mixture into a blender or food processor; purée with buttermilk until mixture is smooth. Sprinkle in basil; stir. Garnish servings with more fresh basil.

Emily Martin, Toronto, Ontario

Beef Burgundy Stew

This classic recipe always brings them to the table quickly.

Makes 10 servings

1 T. canola oil
2 lbs. stew beef cubes
4 slices bacon, crisply cooked and chopped
16-oz. pkg. frozen pearl onions, thawed
8-oz. pkg. mushrooms, quartered
6 redskin potatoes, quartered
2 carrots, peeled and cut into 1/2-inch pieces
14-oz. can beef broth
1 c. low-sodium beef broth
2 T. tomato paste
1 T. fresh thyme, snipped
1/4 t. salt
1/4 t. pepper
3 cloves garlic, minced
2 T. cornstarch
2 t. cold water

Pour oil into a Dutch oven. Brown beef, in batches, until browned on all sides. Add bacon, onions and remaining ingredients except cornstarch and water to Dutch oven. Cover and cook on low heat for one hour or until beef and vegetables are tender. Whisk together cornstarch and water. Stir into stew. Bring to a boil and cook until slightly thickened.

Beef Burgundy Stew

Alice Monaghan, St. Joseph, MO

Oven Beef Stew

This recipe is a lifesaver on busy days...just pop it in the oven and finish up your to-do list!

Serves 6

1-1/2 lbs. stew beef, cubed
5 carrots, peeled and sliced
1 c. celery, chopped
2 onions, sliced
1 potato, peeled and chopped
2 14-1/2 oz. cans stewed tomatoes
1/2 c. soft bread crumbs
2 t. salt
3 T. instant tapioca, uncooked

Place beef, carrots, celery, onions and potato in a bowl. Combine remaining ingredients and add to beef mixture; blend well. Place in a greased 2-1/2 quart Dutch oven. Cover and bake at 325 degrees for 4 hours.

Bev Fisher, Mesa, AZ

Grilled Havarti Sandwiches

Now that my children are grown, I'm always looking for recipes that call for ingredients they wouldn't eat. This sandwich is so tasty, I wanted another one the next day after I first tried it!

Makes 4 sandwiches

8 slices French bread
2 t. butter, softened and divided
1/4 c. apricot preserves
1/4 lb. Havarti cheese, sliced
1 avocado, halved, pitted and sliced

Spread 4 slices bread on one side with half the butter and all the preserves. Top with cheese, avocado and another slice of bread; spread remaining butter on outside of sandwiches. Heat a large cast-iron skillet over medium heat. Cook sandwiches for 2 to 3 minutes, until bread is golden and cheese begins to melt. Turn over; press down slightly with a spatula. Cook until golden.

Grilled Havarti Sandwiches

Cindy Atkins, Vancouver, WA

Creamy Tuna Melts

These open-faced sandwiches are so warm and cozy after an afternoon of sledding or skating.

Makes 8 servings

2 to 3 stalks celery, diced
1 onion, diced
12-oz. can tuna, drained
1/2 c. cottage cheese
1/2 c. mayonnaise
1/4 t. garlic salt
1/8 t. sugar
4 English muffins, split and toasted
8 slices American cheese

In a lightly greased cast-iron skillet, sauté celery and onion until tender. Add tuna, cottage cheese, mayonnaise, garlic salt and sugar to skillet. Mix well, breaking up tuna. Cook over low heat until warmed through, stirring frequently. Remove from heat. Place toasted muffins cut-side up on a broiler pan. Spread with tuna mixture; top with cheese slices. Broil until cheese melts.

Carol Donnelly, San Bernardino, CA

French Onion Soup with Toasted Rye & Gruyère

Makes 4 servings

1/4 c. butter
4 large sweet onions, halved
    crosswise and thinly sliced
1 T. sugar
1/2 t. salt
1/2 t. pepper
3 14-oz. cans beef broth
Optional: 2 T. port or sherry
4 1/2-inch-thick slices rye
    bread, toasted
1 c. shredded Gruyère cheese

Melt butter in a large Dutch oven over medium-high heat. Add onions; cook, uncovered, 20 minutes or until onions are soft, stirring occasionally. Sprinkle sugar over onions; cook over medium heat 10 minutes or until onions are slightly caramelized, stirring occasionally. Stir in salt and pepper; add half of broth and cook, uncovered, 10 minutes. Add remaining broth and, if desired, port; cook 10 more minutes. Ladle soup into 4 oven-proof soup bowls; top each with a slice of toasted rye bread. Sprinkle cheese evenly over bread. Place soup bowls on a baking sheet; broil 5-1/2 inches from heat for 2 minutes or just until cheese melts.

French Onion Soup with Toasted Rye & Gruyère

Jo Cline, Smithville, MO

Sausage Bean Gumbo

Quick & easy...ready in 30 minutes!

Serves 8

14-oz. smoked pork sausage link, sliced
3 15-1/2 oz. cans Great Northern beans
14-1/2 oz. can diced tomatoes with sweet onions
1 stalk celery, diced
1/2 c. green pepper, diced
1/2 t. garlic powder
1/4 t. pepper
Optional: fresh cilantro, chopped

In a Dutch oven over low heat, combine all ingredients except garnish. Do not drain cans. Cover and simmer about 30 minutes, stirring occasionally. Sprinkle servings with cilantro, if desired.

Debby Heatwole, Canadian, TX

Rio Grande Green Pork Chili

Makes a wonderful buffet dish served with warm flour tortillas, or spoon over potato-filled burritos...yum!

Makes 14 servings

3 lbs. boneless pork loin, cubed
1 clove garlic, minced
3 T. olive oil
1/3 c. all-purpose flour
2 14-1/2 oz. cans low-sodium beef broth
32-oz. can tomato juice
14-1/2 oz. can crushed tomatoes
7-oz. can diced green chiles
1/4 c. chopped jalapeño peppers
1/3 c. dried parsley
1/4 c. lemon juice
2 t. ground cumin
1 t. sugar
1/4 t. ground cloves

In a Dutch oven over medium heat, sauté pork and garlic in oil. Add flour, stirring until thoroughly mixed. Add remaining ingredients; cover and simmer for about one hour, until pork is tender, stirring as needed. Garnish as desired.

Rio Grande Green Pork Chili

Tammy Burnett, Springfield, MO

Garlicky Green Chili

My boss shared this zingy chili made with pork chops with me. I've found that every time I prepare it, guests ask me for the recipe!

Serves 8

3 lbs. boneless pork chops, cubed
2 T. oil
1/4 c. all-purpose flour
2 T. garlic, minced
salt and pepper to taste
2 4-oz. cans diced green chiles
14-1/2 oz. can chicken broth
16-oz. jar chunky salsa
1 bunch fresh cilantro, chopped
1 t. ground cumin

In a Dutch oven over medium heat, brown pork in oil. Mix in flour; stir for one minute. Add garlic, salt and pepper; cook for 2 minutes. Stir in remaining ingredients; cover and simmer for 45 minutes.

Elaine Slabinski, Monroe Township, NJ

Creamy Asparagus Soup

This soup is so beautiful! Top with freshly steamed asparagus tips for the perfect topper.

Makes 4 servings

1-1/2 lbs. asparagus, trimmed, chopped and divided
14-1/2 oz. can low-sodium chicken broth
1 T. onion, minced
1/4 t. salt
1/4 t. white pepper
1/2 c. 2% milk

Set aside a few asparagus tips for garnish. Combine remaining ingredients except milk in a Dutch oven over medium heat. Bring to a boil; reduce heat and simmer 5 to 7 minutes, or until asparagus is tender. Working in small batches, ladle asparagus mixture into a blender. Add milk slowly and purée. Return mixture to soup pot and heat through without boiling. Steam or microwave reserved asparagus tips just until tender; use to garnish soup.

Creamy Asparagus Soup

Cheryl Donnelly, Arvada, CO

Summer Squash Chowder

I love to serve this rich and creamy soup on cool summer nights with some fresh fruit.

Makes 4 servings

2 t. canola oil
1 onion, finely diced
1 clove garlic, minced
1 red pepper, finely diced
2 T. all-purpose flour
14-1/2 oz. can vegetable broth, divided
5-oz. can evaporated milk
4 zucchini, diced
2 yellow squash, diced
1 c. fresh corn kernels
1/2 t. hot pepper sauce
3/4 t. dried thyme
1/4 t. salt
2 slices bacon, cooked and cut into small pieces
2 T. lemon juice
1/2 c. fresh parsley, finely chopped
1/2 t. pepper

Add oil to a Dutch oven. Add onion, garlic and red pepper and sauté 5 minutes. Sprinkle flour evenly over vegetables and cook one minute. Add 1/2 cup broth, stirring well to blend. Cook over medium heat until thickened. Pour in remaining broth, milk, zucchini, squash, corn, hot sauce, thyme and salt. Bring to a boil. Reduce heat and simmer, covered, 15 minutes, stirring occasionally. Add bacon, lemon juice and parsley. Heat through and add pepper.

Lynda McCormick, Burkburnett, TX

Lynda's Salmon Burgers

My entire family loves these salmon burgers. I usually serve them with fresh berries or pineapple.

Makes 8 servings

1 lb. salmon fillet, skin removed and chopped
1/2 c. red onion, finely chopped
1/4 c. fresh basil, thinly sliced
1/4 t. salt
1/4 t. pepper
1 egg white
1 T. sriracha hot chili sauce
Optional: 1/4 c. panko bread crumbs
8 slices whole-grain bread, toasted and cut in half
Optional: lettuce leaves, tomato slices

In a large bowl, combine salmon, onion, basil and seasonings; mix gently. In a small bowl, whisk together egg white and chili sauce. Add to salmon mixture and stir well to combine. If mixture is too soft, stir in bread crumbs if desired. Form mixture into 8 patties, 1/4-inch thick. Heat a large cast-iron skillet over medium-high heat. Coat pan with non-stick vegetable spray. Add patties to skillet; cook for about 2 to 3 minutes per side. Place patties sandwich-style on toasted wheat bread. Garnish with lettuce and tomato if desired.

Lynda's Salmon Burgers

Vici Randolph, Gaffney, SC

Kielbasa Camp Stew

I love this recipe! It is so simple, but filling and delicious. This stew is terrific with some crusty bread or cornbread!

Makes 6 to 8 servings

1 lb. Kielbasa sausage, cut into 1-inch
   slices
3 14-1/2 oz. cans diced tomatoes
2 12-oz. pkgs. frozen shoepeg corn
4 potatoes, peeled and diced
1/2 head cabbage, coarsely chopped
1 t. Cajun seasoning or other spicy
   seasoning
salt to taste

Combine Kielbasa, undrained tomatoes and remaining ingredients in a Dutch oven; cover with water. Simmer over medium-high heat until potatoes are tender, stirring occasionally, about 30 minutes.

Rita Morgan, Pueblo, CO

Russian Beef Borscht

Serve with a dollop of plain Greek yogurt...there's nothing better on a cold day!

Makes 12 servings

4 c. cabbage, thinly sliced
1-1/2 lbs. beets, peeled and grated
5 carrots, peeled and sliced
1 parsnip, peeled and sliced
1 c. onion, chopped
1 lb. stew beef, cubed
4 cloves garlic, minced
14-1/2 oz. can no-salt diced tomatoes
3 14-1/2 oz. cans low-sodium beef
   broth
1/4 c. lemon juice
1 T. sugar
1 t. pepper
Garnish: plain yogurt, paprika

In a Dutch oven, add ingredients except garnish in order given. Cover and simmer on medium heat for one hour, just until vegetables are tender, stirring often. Stir well before serving. Garnish as desired.

Russian Beef Borscht

Janice Mullins, Kingston, TN

Ham & Bean Soup

Always a welcome meal after a chilly day in the football stands watching the game!

Makes 6 to 8 servings

1 c. dried navy beans
8 c. water, divided
2 stalks celery, sliced
2 carrots, peeled and sliced
1 onion, chopped
3/4 c. cooked ham, cubed
1 cube chicken bouillon
1 t. dried thyme
2 bay leaves
1/4 t. pepper

In a Dutch oven, combine beans and 4 cups water. Bring to a boil; reduce heat to low. Simmer, uncovered, for 2 minutes. Remove from heat. Cover; let stand for one hour. Drain and rinse beans; return to pan. Add remaining water and other ingredients. Bring to a boil; reduce heat to low. Cover and simmer for 1-1/2 hours, or until beans are tender. Discard bay leaves. Using a fork, slightly mash some of the beans against the side of the pan to thicken soup.

Wendy Reaume, Ontario, Canada

West African Chicken Soup

I had a friend long ago who used to make this delicious soup with flavors of tomato, chicken and curry. It's always been well-loved by all.

Makes 6 servings

2 boneless, skinless chicken breasts, cubed
1 c. onion, chopped
1 T. garlic, minced
1 T. olive oil
1-1/2 t. curry powder
1/2 t. pepper
28-oz. can stewed tomatoes
3 c. low-sodium chicken broth
3 T. creamy peanut butter
3 T. no-salt tomato paste
Garnish: chopped peanuts

In a Dutch oven over medium heat, combine chicken, onion, garlic and olive oil. Sauté until chicken is golden and juices run clear when pierced. Stir in seasonings; cook for another minute. Stir in tomatoes with juice and remaining ingredients. Reduce heat to low; cover and simmer for 10 to 15 minutes. Garnish as desired.

West African Chicken Soup

Rosie Sabo, Toledo, OH

Rainy-Day Tomato Soup

Topped with buttery fresh-baked croutons, here is a modern take on a classic comfort food.

Serves 4

2 T. olive oil
1 onion, thinly sliced
3 to 4 T. garlic, chopped
1 c. celery, chopped
1/2 c. carrot, peeled and cut into
    2-inch sticks
28-oz. can crushed tomatoes
2-1/2 c. vegetable broth
2 t. dried basil
1 t. dried thyme

Heat oil in a Dutch oven over medium heat; add onion and garlic and sauté until onion is translucent. Add celery and carrot; cook 5 more minutes. Add remaining ingredients and bring to a boil. Cover, reduce heat and simmer 1-1/2 hours or until thickened. Ladle soup into 4 bowls; top with Italian Croutons.

Italian Croutons:
1 loaf day-old bread, crusts removed
1/2 c. butter, melted
1 T. Italian seasoning

Cube bread and place in a large plastic zipping bag; set aside. Combine butter and seasoning; pour over bread. Mix well; arrange bread cubes on an ungreased baking sheet. Bake at 425 degrees for 10 minutes; turn bread cubes and bake 5 more minutes.

Carol Lytle, Columbus, OH

Carol's Veggie Panini

You can add a thin slice of deli turkey to this panini for those meat lovers in your family.

Makes 4 servings

2 T. balsamic vinegar
1 T. olive oil
1/8 t. salt
1/8 t. pepper
1 eggplant, cut into 1/4-inch slices
1 zucchini, cut into 8 slices
1/2 red pepper, quartered
8 slices whole-grain bread
1/2 c. shredded, part-skim
    mozzarella cheese
8 fresh basil leaves

Whisk vinegar, oil, salt and pepper in a bowl; set aside. Spray a baking sheet with non-stick vegetable spray. Brush both sides of eggplant and zucchini with vinegar mixture. Arrange in a single layer on baking sheet. Coat all vegetables with vegetable spray. Broil about 4 inches from heat for 7 to 8 minutes, turning once and coating vegetables with spray as needed. Lightly brush one side of each bread slice with remaining vinegar mixture; turn and coat second side with spray. Place bread, sprayed-side down, on an ungreased baking sheet. Top with vegetables, cheese and basil. Top with remaining bread slices, sprayed-side up. Place sandwiches, one at a time, in a cast-iron skillet; set a bacon press or other weight on top. Cook sandwiches over medium-high heat for about 4 minutes, turning once, until lightly golden on both sides.

Carol's Veggie Panini

Susan Buetow, Du Quoin, IL

Buffalo Chicken Sandwich

Besides looking tasty, this sandwich is very easy to make. It's my go-to recipe when hubby is having buddies over!

Makes 6 sandwiches

6 boneless chicken breasts
1 onion, chopped
6 stalks celery, chopped
2 to 3 T. olive oil
1/2 c. all-purpose flour
Optional: 1 t. seasoning salt
17-1/2-oz. bottle buffalo wing sauce
6 soft buns, split
Garnish: ranch or blue cheese salad
    dressing, crumbled blue cheese,
    additional wing sauce

Flatten chicken breasts to 1/4-inch thin between pieces of wax paper; set aside. In a cast-iron skillet over medium-low heat, sauté onion and celery in oil until tender. In a shallow bowl, combine flour and seasoning salt, if using. Dredge chicken pieces in flour mixture. Add chicken on top of onion mixture in pan. Cook for 5 minutes; flip chicken and cook an additional 5 minutes. Add buffalo wing sauce to pan. Cover; increase heat to medium, and cook 5 to 7 minutes, until chicken juices run clear. Serve on buns; garnish as desired.

Lisa Lankins, Mazatlán, Mexico

Chicken, Lime & Tortilla Soup

This is such a delicious soup, I hope you try it!

Makes 8 servings

3 lbs. chicken
2 tomatoes, chopped
1 jalapeño pepper, chopped
1/4 c. fresh cilantro, chopped
juice of 3 limes
2 t. Worcestershire sauce
1 onion, chopped
1/2 c. red pepper, chopped
1/4 c. fresh or frozen corn
1/4 c. brown rice, uncooked
1 t. chopped green chiles
1 t. garlic, minced
1/2 t. pepper
1/4 t. salt
Garnish: diced avocado, shredded
    Mexican-blend cheese, tortilla
    strips

Cover chicken with water in a Dutch oven. Bring to a boil over medium-high heat. Reduce heat to low; simmer about an hour, or until chicken is very tender and juices run clear when pierced. Remove chicken to a plate, reserving 4 cups broth in pot. Let chicken cool slightly. Add tomatoes, jalapeño, cilantro, lime juice and Worcestershire sauce to reserved broth; simmer 45 minutes. Meanwhile, chop half the chicken and set aside; reserve the rest for another recipe. Stir remaining ingredients except garnish into soup; simmer 20 more minutes. Stir in chopped chicken. Garnish individual servings as desired.

Chicken, Lime & Tortilla Soup

Lea Ann Burwell, Charles Town, WV

Ranch Chicken Wraps

Makes 8 to 10 wraps

1/2 t. oil
4 boneless, skinless chicken breasts,
 cut into strips
2.8-oz. can French-fried onions
1/4 c. bacon bits
8-oz. pkg. shredded Cheddar cheese
lettuce leaves
8 to 10 8-inch flour tortillas
Garnish: ranch salad dressing

Heat oil in a large cast-iron skillet over medium heat. Add chicken and cook until chicken is golden and juices run clear when chicken is pierced. Add onions, bacon bits and cheese to skillet; cook until cheese melts. Place several lettuce leaves on each tortilla and spoon chicken mixture down center; roll up. Serve with ranch salad dressing.

Stephanie Jenkins, McKinney, TX

Spicy Chicken Soup

This zesty, fresh soup is my husband's absolute favorite! When he was living in Guatemala as a missionary, I taught him how to make it, and he made it every week. Now, a bowl of this soup brings back memories for him.

Makes 6 servings

1 lb. chicken breasts and/or thighs
1 onion, chopped
1 jalapeño pepper, seeded and
 minced
4 cloves garlic, minced
4 carrots, peeled and thinly sliced
8 c. water
1/4 t. salt
1/4 t. pepper
3/4 c. long-cooking brown rice,
 uncooked
Garnish: lime wedges, avocado
 slices, shredded Monterey Jack
 cheese

In a Dutch oven over medium-high heat, combine all ingredients except rice and garnish. Bring to a boil; reduce heat to medium-low. Simmer, partially covered, for 45 minutes, or until chicken juices run clear. Remove chicken and set aside to cool, reserving broth in soup pot. Return broth to a boil; stir in rice. Reduce heat to low and simmer, covered, for 45 minutes, or until rice is tender. Meanwhile, shred chicken, discarding skin and bones. When rice is tender, return chicken to the pot and heat through. Serve soup in large bowls, garnished with a squeeze of lime juice, a few slices of avocado and a sprinkling of cheese.

Spicy Chicken Soup

Kathy McCann-Neff, Claxton, GA

Chill-Chaser Pork Stew

After a day of raking leaves, this stew warms and rejuvenates you!

Serves 6

2 to 2-1/2 lbs. pork steaks, cubed
2 T. olive oil
2 sweet onions, chopped
2 green peppers, chopped
2 cloves garlic, minced
salt and pepper to taste
6-oz. can tomato paste
28-oz. can diced tomatoes
2 8-oz. cans sliced mushrooms, drained

In a Dutch oven over medium heat, sauté pork in oil until browned. Add onions, green peppers, garlic, salt and pepper. Cover; cook over medium heat until pork is tender. Add tomato paste, tomatoes with juice and mushrooms; bring to a boil. Reduce heat to low; simmer for one hour, stirring often.

Lyuba Brooke, Jacksonville, FL

Chicken, Wild Rice & Mushroom Soup

A new twist on an old recipe I had for chicken rice soup. The wild rice gives it such a nice flavor! The recipe may seem lengthy at first glance, but it's mostly simmering time...perfect for a cozy weekend.

Makes 10 servings

4 chicken breasts
9 c. water
3 cloves garlic, minced
1 T. butter
2 shallots, sliced
1-1/2 c. baby portabella mushrooms, sliced
1/2 c. wild rice, uncooked
1/2 c. milk
1/2 t. salt
1/2 t. pepper
Garnish: sliced shallots

Combine chicken and water in a Dutch oven. Bring to a boil over medium-high heat; reduce heat to low. Cover and simmer for 60 to 90 minutes. Remove chicken to a bowl, reserving broth. Let chicken cool. Meanwhile, in a large stockpot over medium heat, sauté garlic in butter until fragrant. Add shallots and mushrooms; cook until almost tender. Add rice; cook and stir for 2 to 3 minutes. Add 7 cups reserved broth. Bring to a boil; reduce heat to medium-low. Cover and cook, stirring occasionally, for 20 minutes. Dice chicken, discarding skin and bones; add chicken to soup. Cover and simmer for 15 to 20 minutes, until most of broth is absorbed. If more liquid is needed, add remaining broth, one cup at a time, to desired consistency. Stir in milk, salt and pepper; bring to a boil. Reduce heat to medium-low and simmer for another 15 to 20 minutes. Garnish as desired.

Chicken, Wild Rice & Mushroom Soup

Charlotte Orm, Florence, AZ

California Avocado Soup

This soup is so pretty and makes a lovely luncheon soup any time of the year.

Serves 6

1/2 c. onion, chopped
1 T. butter
2 14-1/2 oz. cans chicken broth
2 potatoes, peeled and cubed
1/2 t. salt
1/4 t. pepper
2 ripe avocados, halved and pitted
Garnish: sour cream, real bacon bits

In a Dutch oven over medium heat, sauté onion in butter until tender. Add broth, potatoes, salt and pepper; bring to a boil. Reduce heat to low. Cover and simmer for 15 to 25 minutes, until potatoes are tender. Remove from heat; cool slightly. Working in batches, scoop avocado pulp into a blender; add potato mixture with broth. Cover and process until puréed. Return to pan; heat through. Garnish with sour cream and bacon bits.

Kathy Grashoff, Fort Wayne, IN

Curried Harvest Bisque

Top with ham for an elegant beginning to a holiday meal.

Serves 4

1 lb. butternut squash, peeled and
    cut into 1-inch cubes
5 c. chicken broth
1/4 c. butter
1/4 c. all-purpose flour
1 t. curry powder
3/4 c. half-and-half
1 T. lime juice
1/2 t. salt
1/4 t. white pepper
Garnish: diced cooked ham

Combine squash and broth in a 4-quart Dutch oven. Cook over medium heat until squash is tender, about 15 minutes. Using a slotted spoon, transfer squash to a blender; process until smooth. Add broth to squash; set aside. Melt butter in Dutch oven; stir in flour and curry powder. Cook over medium heat, stirring until smooth. Add squash mixture; increase heat to medium-high and stir until soup thickens slightly. Reduce heat to low; add remaining ingredients except garnish and heat through without boiling. Garnish with ham.

Curried Harvest Bisque

Elijah Dahlstrom, Ames, IA

Easy Tomato Soup

Other tasty additions to try...chopped fresh basil, chopped fresh chives, chopped fresh rosemary, croutons, freshly grated Parmesan cheese and grated lemon zest.

Serves 8 to 10

28-oz. can Italian-seasoned diced
   tomatoes
26-oz. can tomato soup
32-oz. container chicken broth
1/2 t. pepper
Optional: sour cream, chopped fresh
   basil

Pulse tomatoes in a food processor or blender 3 to 4 times, or until finely diced. Stir together tomatoes, soup, chicken broth and pepper in a Dutch oven. Cook over medium heat, stirring occasionally, for 10 minutes, or until thoroughly heated. Top servings with sour cream and chopped fresh basil, if desired.

Arleena Connor, Leopold, IN

Toasted Ham & Cheese

Serve these buttery sandwiches with a side of potato chips and a crisp dill pickle, or a cup of tomato bisque. Pure comfort!

Serves 4

2-1/2 T. butter, softened
8 slices sourdough bread
4 slices Colby cheese
1/2 lb. shaved deli ham
4 slices Swiss cheese

Spread butter on one side of each slice of bread. Arrange 4 bread slices, buttered-side down, in a cast-iron skillet over medium-high heat. Top with one slice Colby cheese, desired amount of ham and one slice Swiss cheese. Add remaining bread slices, buttered-side up. Grill sandwiches on both sides until golden and cheese melts.

FLAVOR BOOST
Add a little kick to this cheese sandwich by spreading some pesto on the bread before adding the cheese. Yummy!

Toasted Ham & Cheese

Sandy Westendorp, Grand Rapids, MI

Pumpkin Chowder

This blend of everyday ingredients is anything but ordinary.

Serves 6

1/2 lb. bacon, diced
2 c. onion, chopped
2 t. curry powder
2 T. all-purpose flour
1-lb. pie pumpkin, peeled, seeded
    and chopped
2 potatoes, peeled and cubed
4 c. chicken broth
1 c. half-and-half
salt and pepper to taste
Garnish: toasted pumpkin seeds,
    sliced green onions

Brown bacon in a Dutch oven over medium heat for 5 minutes; add onion. Sauté for 10 minutes; add curry powder and flour, stirring until smooth and creamy, about 5 minutes. Add pumpkin, potatoes and broth; simmer until pumpkin and potatoes are tender, about 15 minutes. Pour in half-and-half; season with salt and pepper. Simmer for 5 minutes; do not boil. Spoon into soup bowls; garnish with pumpkin seeds and green onions.

Stacie Avner, Delaware, OH

Nacho Burgers

This is just about the best burger you'll ever eat! The avocado topping makes it a hit every time. And the chips in the meat mixture adds so much flavor. My kids ask for this burger more than any other!

Serves 5

1 small avocado, pitted, peeled
    and diced
1 plum tomato, diced
2 green onions, chopped
2 t. lime juice
1-1/4 lbs. lean ground beef
1 egg, beaten
3/4 c. nacho-flavored tortilla chips,
    crushed
1/4 c. fresh cilantro, chopped
1/2 t. chili powder
1/2 t. ground cumin
salt and pepper to taste
1-1/4 c. shredded Pepper Jack cheese
5 whole-wheat hamburger buns,
    split

Mix together avocado, tomato, onions and lime juice; mash slightly and set aside. Combine beef, egg, chips and seasonings in a large bowl. Form into 5 patties. Heat a cast-iron skillet over medium heat. Cook to desired doneness, turning to cook on both sides. Sprinkle cheese over burgers; grill until melted. Serve on buns; spread with avocado mixture.

Nacho Burgers

Robin Cornett, Spring Hill, FL

Cape Cod Clam Chowder

For smoky flavor, stir in some crisply cooked and crumbled bacon.

Serves 6 to 8

2 10-3/4 oz. cans New England
    clam chowder
10-3/4 oz. can cream of celery soup
10-3/4 oz. can cream of potato soup
2 pts. half-and-half
3 potatoes, peeled and diced
salt and pepper to taste
Optional: chopped fresh chives

Combine soups and half-and-half in a Dutch oven. Cook over medium-low heat until heated through, stirring often. Set aside over low heat. Boil potatoes in water for about 10 minutes; drain and add to soup mixture. Cook over medium heat until potatoes are tender. Add salt and pepper to taste. Garnish with chives, if desired.

Robyn Fiedler, Tacoma, WA

Turkey-Vegetable Chowder

This is a terrific, hearty chowder made using your leftover turkey!

Makes 8 cups

1/4 c. butter
2 onions, chopped
2 T. all-purpose flour
1 t. curry powder
3 c. chicken broth
1 potato, peeled and chopped
1 c. carrots, peeled and thinly sliced
1 c. celery, thinly sliced
2 T. fresh parsley, minced
1/2 t. dried sage or poultry seasoning
3 c. cooked turkey, chopped
1-1/2 c. half-and-half
10-oz. pkg. frozen chopped spinach
Optional: fresh parsley leaves

Melt butter in a small Dutch oven. Add onions and sauté 10 minutes. Stir in flour and curry powder. Cook 2 minutes. Add broth, potato, carrots, celery, parsley and sage. Reduce heat to low. Cover and simmer 10 to 15 minutes. Add turkey, half-and-half and frozen spinach. Cover and simmer, stirring occasionally, for 10 minutes or until heated through. Garnish with fresh parsley leaves, if desired.

Turkey-Vegetable Chowder

Penny Sherman, Ava, MO

Creamy Pumpkin Soup

This soup is a wonderful way to use up some leftover pumpkin. And for dessert, serve up big slices of pumpkin pie with generous dollops of whipped cream!

Serves 6

2 T. oil
1 lb. beef short ribs
4 c. water
3 c. pumpkin, peeled and chopped
1 baking potato, peeled and cubed
1 carrot, peeled and chopped
1 onion, chopped
salt and pepper to taste

Heat oil in a Dutch oven over medium heat. Brown ribs in oil; drain. Stir in water and bring to a boil. Reduce heat and simmer, covered, one hour. Remove short ribs from Dutch oven, cut off meat and shred; set aside. Stir remaining ingredients into Dutch oven. Simmer, covered, for 45 minutes. Pour half the soup into a blender and process until smooth. Repeat with remaining soup. Stir in reserved beef. Return to Dutch oven and heat through before serving.

Carol Field Dahlstrom, Ankeny, IA

Garbanzo Bean Soup

Everyone loves this healthy, easy-to-make soup. If you are eating gluten-free, use quinoa instead of orzo.

Serves 8

2 T. olive oil
1 small onion, chopped
1 red pepper, chopped
2 boneless, skinless chicken breasts
14-1/2 oz. can petite diced tomatoes, undrained, or 1-1/2 cups peeled and diced fresh tomatoes
2 c. chicken broth
1/2 c. orzo
15.8-oz. can garbanzo beans, rinsed and drained
2 tablespoons chopped fresh cilantro
1 c. frozen or fresh corn
Optional: sliced avocado, chopped fresh cilantro

In a Dutch oven, heat oil over medium heat. Add onion and red pepper; place chicken breasts on top. Sauté for 7 to 8 minutes, turning chicken once. Remove chicken to a plate; set aside. Add tomatoes and broth; bring to a boil. Add orzo and cook for 5 minutes or until orzo is tender. Add beans, cilantro and corn; cook for 10 minutes. Shred chicken; stir into soup and heat. Garnish with avocado and cilantro, if desired.

Garbanzo Bean Soup

Shrimp with Pesto, Corn & Tomatoes, p. 126

CHAPTER THREE

QUICK-TO-FIX
Mains

Creamy Chicken Spaghetti, p. 162

Aunt Judy's Macaroni & Cheese, p. 122

Lisa Windhorn, Seattle, WA

Maple Pot Roast

I love making this dish for a special fall meal...all the meat and veggies in one pot!

Makes 4 to 6 servings

2-lb. boneless beef chuck roast
1/2 c. orange juice
1/2 c. maple syrup
2 T. red wine vinegar
1 T. Worcestershire sauce
2 t. orange zest
1/4 t. salt
1/4 t. pepper
2 carrots, peeled and cut into 2-inch
 pieces
2 stalks celery, cut into 2-inch pieces
1 onion, chopped
2 potatoes, peeled and cut into
 2-inch cubes

Brown roast over medium heat in a Dutch oven sprayed with non-stick vegetable spray. In a bowl, combine orange juice, syrup, vinegar, Worcestershire sauce, orange zest, salt and pepper. Pour over roast. Bring to a boil. Reduce heat; cover and simmer one hour. Add carrots, celery and onions; cover and simmer 20 minutes. Add potatoes; cover and simmer for 20 minutes, until tender.

Wendy Knowles, Pittsfield, ME

Chicken Cacciatore

This delicious recipe is easy to double. Try using Italian-seasoned diced tomatoes for even more flavor.

Makes 4 to 6 servings

2 lbs. chicken pieces
2 T. oil
14-1/2 oz. can diced tomatoes
28-oz. jar spaghetti sauce
1 green pepper, sliced
1 onion, chopped
2 cloves garlic, minced
1 t. Italian seasoning
salt and pepper to taste
cooked pasta or rice
Garnish: grated Parmesan cheese

In a cast-iron Dutch oven or skillet over medium heat, brown chicken in oil. Drain; stir in tomatoes with juice and remaining ingredients except cheese. Reduce heat to medium-low. Cover and simmer until chicken juices run clear when pierced and vegetables are tender, stirring occasionally. Serve over cooked pasta or rice, topped with Parmesan cheese.

Chicken Cacciatore

Staci Prickett, Montezuma, GA

Stuffed Beer Brats

I got this recipe from my dad. He didn't often cook for us, but when he did, dinner always seemed extra delicious.

Serves 6

1/4 c. butter, sliced
1 onion, sliced
6 bratwurst sausages
12-oz. can regular or non-alcoholic beer
15-oz. can sauerkraut, drained
6 slices bacon
6 hot dog buns, split
Garnish: Swiss cheese slices, horseradish mustard

Melt butter in a Dutch oven over medium heat. Add onion; cook for 3 minutes. Add brats and beer; bring to a boil. Reduce heat; simmer for 5 to 10 minutes. Remove brats to a plate, reserving beer mixture. Cut a V-shaped notch lengthwise in brats. Stuff with sauerkraut; wrap with bacon and fasten with a wooden toothpick. Grill over medium heat until golden and bacon is crisp. Return brats to beer mixture until served. Serve on buns, garnished as desired.

Deb Eaton, Mesa, AZ

Deb's Chicken Florentine

My husband loves Italian food! When a local restaurant closed, he was sad that he couldn't get his favorite dish anymore, so I recreated it for him at home. You can substitute frozen spinach, canned mushrooms or leftover rotisserie chicken.

Makes 6 servings

16-oz. pkg. linguine pasta, uncooked
2 T. olive oil
3 cloves garlic, minced
4 boneless, skinless chicken breasts, thinly sliced
1-1/4 c. zesty Italian salad dressing, divided
8 sun-dried tomatoes, chopped
8-oz. pkg. sliced mushrooms
5-oz. pkg. baby spinach
cracked pepper to taste
Optional: grated Parmesan cheese

Cook pasta according to package directions; drain. While pasta is cooking, warm oil in a cast-iron skillet over medium heat. Add garlic and cook 2 minutes. Add chicken; cook until no longer pink. Drizzle chicken with one cup salad dressing. Stir in tomatoes and mushrooms; cover skillet and simmer until mushrooms are softened. Add spinach; cover skillet again. Cook another 2 to 3 minutes, just until spinach is wilted; stir and sprinkle with pepper. Toss cooked linguine with remaining salad dressing. Serve chicken and vegetables over linguine; garnish as desired.

Deb's Chicken Florentine

Cyndi Little, Whitsett, NC

Buttermilk Fried Chicken

My daddy made amazing fried chicken, but he passed away when I was 12. It's taken me a long time to make chicken that I feel is almost as good as his.

Serves 4 to 6

2-1/2 lbs. chicken
1 c. buttermilk
1 c. all-purpose flour
1-1/2 t. salt
1/2 t. pepper
oil for frying

Combine chicken and buttermilk in a large bowl. Cover and refrigerate for one hour. Meanwhile, combine flour, salt and pepper in a large plastic zipping bag. Drain chicken, discarding buttermilk. Working in batches, add chicken to bag and toss to coat. Shake off excess flour and let chicken rest for 15 minutes. Heat 1/4 inch of oil in a large cast-iron skillet over medium heat. Fry chicken in oil until golden on all sides. Reduce heat to medium-low; cover and simmer, turning occasionally, for 40 to 45 minutes, until juices run clear. Uncover and cook 5 minutes longer.

Linda Kilgore, Kittanning, PA

Deep-Dish Skillet Pizza

This recipe is my husband's. He made us one of these pizzas for supper and now it's the only pizza we ever want to eat. Delicious!

Serves 4

1 loaf frozen bread dough, thawed
15-oz. jar pizza sauce
1/2 lb. ground pork sausage, browned and drained
5-oz. pkg. sliced pepperoni
1/2 c. sliced mushrooms
1/2 c. green pepper, sliced
Italian seasoning to taste
1 c. shredded mozzarella cheese
1 c. shredded Cheddar cheese

Generously grease a large cast-iron skillet. Press thawed dough into the bottom and up the sides of skillet. Spread desired amount of pizza sauce over dough. Add favorite toppings, ending with cheeses on top. Bake at 425 degrees for 30 minutes. Carefully remove skillet from oven. Let stand several minutes; pizza will finish baking in the skillet. Slice and serve.

Deep-Dish Skillet Pizza

Maria Kuhna, Crofton, MD

Too-Much-Zucchini Stovetop Dinner

A scrumptious hearty dish for when your garden is overflowing with zucchini!

Serves 6 to 8

3 c. elbow macaroni, uncooked
2 T. olive oil
1 onion, chopped
2 cloves garlic, minced
1 lb. ground beef
1/2 lb. ground Italian pork sausage
3 to 4 zucchini, quartered and sliced
    1/2-inch thick
14-1/2 oz. can crushed tomatoes
26-oz. jar spaghetti sauce
6-oz. can tomato paste
1/2 c. water
1/2 t. dried basil
1/2 t. dried oregano
1/2 t. garlic powder
salt and pepper to taste
8-oz. pkg. shredded mozzarella
    cheese

Cook macaroni according to package directions; drain. Meanwhile, add oil to a large cast-iron skillet over medium heat. Sauté onion and garlic until tender, about 5 minutes. Add beef and sausage; cook until browned. Drain; stir in zucchini, tomatoes with juice and remaining ingredients except mozzarella cheese. Cover and simmer for 10 to 15 minutes, until zucchini is tender. Add seasonings; top with cheese. Serve zucchini mixture ladled over cooked macaroni.

Judy Young, Plano, TX

Lemon Wine Chicken Skillet

This is one of my family's all-time favorite chicken recipes. It is so easy to make and tastes phenomenal! Serve with steamed brown rice or your favorite pasta.

Serves 4

4 boneless, skinless chicken breasts
lemon pepper to taste
1 egg
1/2 c. lemon-flavored white cooking
    wine, divided
1/4 c. all-purpose flour
6 T. butter, divided
2 to 3 T. capers
Garnish: chopped fresh parsley

Flatten chicken breasts slightly between 2 pieces of wax paper. Season chicken with lemon pepper. In a small bowl, lightly beat egg with 2 tablespoons wine. Place flour in a separate shallow bowl. Dip chicken in egg mixture, then in flour to coat. Melt 3 tablespoons butter in a large cast-iron skillet over medium heat; add chicken. Cook until golden on both sides and no longer pink in the center, about 6 minutes on each side. Transfer chicken to a serving dish. Add remaining wine and butter to drippings in skillet; cook and stir until butter melts. Add capers; heat through. To serve, spoon sauce from the skillet over chicken; sprinkle with parsley.

Lemon Wine Chicken Skillet

Emma Brown, Saskatchewan, Canada

Maple Pork Chops

The sweetness of the maple syrup and saltiness of the soy sauce go together so well, you may want to double this recipe!

Makes 4 servings

1/2 c. maple syrup
3 T. soy sauce
2 cloves garlic, minced
4 thick bone-in pork chops
1 T. oil

In a bowl, whisk together maple syrup, soy sauce and garlic; reserve and refrigerate 1/4 cup of mixture. Add pork chops to remaining mixture in bowl. Cover and refrigerate for at least 15 minutes to overnight, turning pork chops occasionally. Drain, discarding mixture in bowl. Heat oil in a large cast-iron skillet over medium-high heat. Add pork chops. Cook until golden and no longer pink in the center, about 5 minutes per side. At serving time, warm reserved syrup mixture; drizzle over pork chops.

Judy Croll, Rowlett, TX

Aunt Judy's Macaroni & Cheese

My family always requests this comforting dish for special holiday gatherings. It is so simple to prepare, and delicious with baked ham or just by itself. There are never any leftovers.

Serves 8 to 10

8-oz. pkg. elbow macaroni, uncooked
2 T. oil
1 T. plus 1 t. salt, divided
1/4 c. butter
1/3 c. all-purpose flour
3 c. milk, warmed
1/2 t. pepper
8-oz. pkg. pasteurized process
    cheese, cubed
1/2 c. shredded Cheddar cheese

Cook macaroni according to package directions, adding oil and one tablespoon salt to cooking water; drain and set aside. Meanwhile, melt butter in a Dutch oven over medium heat. Add flour; cook and stir for 3 minutes, or until bubbly. Do not brown. Whisk in warm milk and bring to a boil, stirring constantly. Add remaining salt, pepper and cubed cheese. Stir until cheese is melted; remove from heat. Add cooked macaroni to cheese sauce and stir. Bake, uncovered, at 350 degrees for 20 to 30 minutes, until bubbly. Top with shredded cheese; return to oven just until cheese melts.

Aunt Judy's Macaroni & Cheese

Flo Burtnett, Gage, OK

One-Pot Spaghetti

Nothing could be easier! I make this at least one night a week when time is short...it disappears fast!

Makes 4 servings

1 lb. ground beef
1 onion, diced
2 14-oz. cans chicken broth
6-oz. can tomato paste
1/2 t. dried oregano
1/2 t. salt
1/4 t. pepper
1/8 t. garlic powder
8-oz. pkg. spaghetti, uncooked and
    broken
Garnish: grated Parmesan cheese

Brown ground beef and onion in a large cast-iron skillet over medium heat. Drain; return to skillet. Stir in broth, tomato paste and seasonings; bring to a boil. Add spaghetti; reduce heat and simmer, stirring often, cooking for about 15 minutes, or until spaghetti is tender. Sprinkle with cheese.

Shelley Turner, Boise, ID

Homemade Fish Sticks

My kids love these yummy fish sticks! I serve them in diner-style baskets with French fries.

Makes 8 servings

2 lbs. cod fillets
2 eggs
2 T. water
salt and pepper to taste
1-1/2 c. seasoned dry bread crumbs
3 T. grated Parmesan cheese
1/4 c. olive oil
1/2 c. tartar sauce
Optional: lemon wedges

Cut fish into 4-inch by one-inch strips; set aside. In a shallow dish, beat together egg, water and seasonings. In a separate dish, mix bread crumbs and cheese. Dip fish into egg mixture; coat with bread crumb mixture and set aside. Heat olive oil in a cast-iron skillet over medium-high heat. Working in batches, add fish to skillet and cook until flaky and golden, about 3 minutes per side. Drain fish sticks on paper towels. Serve with tartar sauce and lemon wedges, if desired.

Homemade Fish Sticks

Pat Crandall, Rochester, NY

Rustic Kielbasa Skillet

This is one of my husband's favorite quick-cook meals, so I make it often. A hearty country bread completes the meal.

Serves 3 to 4

12 new redskin potatoes, quartered
1 to 2 onions, quartered
1 green pepper, diced
1 T. olive oil
3/4 c. chicken broth
2 T. soy sauce
1-1/2 lbs. Kielbasa sausage, sliced
  1/2-inch thick

In a large cast-iron skillet over medium heat, cook potatoes, onions and pepper in oil until potatoes are golden. Add broth and soy sauce; cook until potatoes and vegetables are fork-tender. Toss in Kielbasa and cook until heated through.

Carol Field Dahlstrom, Ankeny, IA

Shrimp with Pesto, Corn & Tomatoes

Such a beautiful summer dish using fresh corn and tomatoes!

Serves 4

2 thick-cut bacon slices, chopped
4 c. fresh corn kernels, cut from cob
2 c. cherry tomatoes, halved
2 T. refrigerated basil pesto
1/2 t. salt
1/4 t. pepper
8 large shrimp, peeled and deveined
1 T. olive oil

Cook bacon in a large cast-iron skillet over medium-high, stirring occasionally, until fat is rendered and bacon is crisp, about 6 minutes. Transfer to a plate, reserving one tablespoon drippings in skillet. Add corn kernels; cook, stirring often, until tender-crisp, about 4 minutes. Remove skillet from heat; stir in cherry tomatoes, pesto, salt and pepper. Transfer to a medium bowl; cover to keep warm. Wipe skillet clean. Heat oil in skillet over medium-high. Add shrimp and cook until pink and cooked through, about 5 minutes. Add to corn mixture.

Shrimp with Pesto, Corn & Tomatoes

Lorena Freis, Waterloo, IA

Seafood Fettuccine

Scallops or crabmeat may be substituted for variety.

Makes 4 servings

3/4 lb. shrimp, cooked, peeled and
    deveined
4-oz. can mushroom stems and
    pieces, drained
1/2 t. garlic powder
1/8 t. salt
1/8 t. pepper
1/4 c. butter
8-oz. pkg. fettuccine, cooked and
    drained
1/2 c. grated Parmesan cheese
1/2 c. milk
1/2 c. sour cream
Garnish: 1/2 T. fresh parsley,
    chopped

In a large cast-iron skillet over medium-high heat, sauté shrimp, mushrooms and seasonings in butter for 3 to 5 minutes. Stir in fettuccine, Parmesan cheese, milk and sour cream. Cook over medium heat until warmed; do not boil. Garnish with parsley.

Kari Hodges, Jacksonville, TX

Skillet Goulash

I like to serve up this old-fashioned family favorite with thick slices of freshly baked sweet cornbread topped with pats of butter.

Makes 8 to 10 servings

2 lbs. ground beef
10-oz. can diced tomatoes with
    green chiles
14-1/2 oz. can stewed tomatoes
6 baking potatoes, peeled and diced
15-oz. can tomato sauce
15-1/2 oz. can corn, drained
14-1/2 oz. can ranch-style beans
salt and pepper to taste
Garnish: shredded cheese

Brown beef in a Dutch oven over medium heat; drain. Add tomatoes with juice and remaining ingredients; reduce heat. Cover and simmer until potatoes are tender and mixture has thickened, about 45 minutes. Garnish with shredded cheese.

DID YOU KNOW
Every time you cook in your cast-iron pans, you are making them better by seasoning them. After washing your pans, be sure to dry by hand and oil them lightly.

Skillet Goulash

Amanda Johnson, Marysville, OH

Kickin' Cajun Tilapia

My husband loves this delicious fish dish! Tilapia is a mild, tasty fish, and this recipe really has a flavorful zip.

Serves 4

3 T. paprika
1 T. onion powder
1 t. cayenne pepper
1 t. dried thyme
1 t. dried oregano
1/2 t. celery salt
1/8 t. garlic powder
2 t. salt
2 t. pepper
4 tilapia fillets
2 T. oil
Garnish: lemon wedges

Mix seasonings in a shallow bowl or on a plate. Press both sides of tilapia fillets into seasoning mixture; let stand for 10 minutes. Heat oil in a cast-iron skillet over medium heat. Cook fillets for 4 to 6 minutes, turning once, until fish flakes easily with a fork. Remove fish to a serving plate and garnish with lemon wedges.

Deb Grumbine, Greeley, CO

Deb's Garden Bounty Dinner

I love to make this dish because it is a complete meal in a skillet. My entire family loves it when I serve this for a weeknight dinner.

Makes 6 servings

1 T. oil
6 chicken drumsticks
8 zucchini, chopped
1 lb. mushrooms, chopped
1/2 green pepper, chopped
1/2 red pepper, chopped
1 onion, chopped
2 15-oz. cans stewed tomatoes
2 t. garlic, minced
1 t. turmeric
1/2 t. pepper
2 c. cooked brown rice

Heat oil in a cast-iron skillet over medium-high heat. Add chicken and cook 20 to 25 minutes, or until golden. Set aside and keep warm. Add remaining ingredients except rice to skillet; cook 5 minutes. Return chicken to skillet and continue to cook until juices run clear. Serve alongside servings of rice.

Deb's Garden Bounty Dinner

Vickie, Gooseberry Patch

Boiled Shrimp in Beer

Treat yourself to these super-easy peel & eat shrimp...even clean-up is a snap! Dump shrimp onto a picnic table covered with newspaper, then after dinner, just toss the paper, shells and all.

Serves 4

1 qt. water
12-oz. can regular or non-alcoholic beer
1 lemon, sliced
1 onion, chopped
1 stalk celery, diced
1 T. seafood seasoning
2 bay leaves
hot pepper sauce to taste
1 lb. uncooked large shrimp, cleaned
Garnish: cocktail sauce

Combine all ingredients except shrimp and garnish in a Dutch oven. Bring to a boil over medium-high heat. Add shrimp; cover and return to a full boil for 3 to 4 minutes. Stir; remove from heat. Let stand 3 to 4 additional minutes, until shrimp turn pink. Drain well; discard bay leaves. Serve with cocktail sauce.

Trisha Donley, Pinedale, WY

Skillet Bowtie Lasagna

This is one of my favorite go-to meals. I love to serve it with a fresh green salad and slices of warm, buttered Italian bread.

Serves 4

1 lb. ground beef
1 onion, chopped
1 clove garlic, chopped
14-1/2 oz. can diced tomatoes
1-1/2 c. water
6-oz. can tomato paste
1 T. dried parsley
2 t. dried oregano
1 t. salt
2-1/2 c. bowtie pasta, uncooked
3/4 c. small-curd cottage cheese
1/4 c. grated Parmesan cheese

In a large cast-iron skillet over medium heat, brown beef, onion and garlic; drain. Add tomatoes with juice, water, tomato paste and seasonings; mix well. Stir in pasta; bring to a boil. Reduce heat, cover and simmer for 20 to 25 minutes, until pasta is tender, stirring once. Combine cheeses; drop by rounded tablespoonfuls onto pasta mixture. Cover and cook for 5 minutes.

Skillet Bowtie Lasagna

Dottie Liwai, Durant, OK

Saucy Beef Skillet

This beef comes out so tender...it's absolutely wonderful. Serve over some cooked rice or egg noodles and you've got yourself one tasty meal!

Serves 4

3 T. oyster sauce or soy sauce
1-1/2 T. dry sherry or orange juice
2 t. cornstarch
1/2 t. sugar
2 T. peanut oil
2 lbs. beef round steak, thinly sliced
6 green onions, sliced 1/2-inch long

In a bowl, mix together sauce, sherry or orange juice, cornstarch and sugar; set aside. Heat oil in a large cast-iron skillet over medium heat; add steak and cook for about 3 minutes. Stir in sauce mixture. Add green onions and cook for an additional 10 minutes, or until steak is cooked through and onions are tender.

Vickie, Gooseberry Patch

Rosemary Pork & Mushrooms

This simple dish is delicious with ordinary button mushrooms, but for a special dinner I'll use a combination of wild mushrooms...their earthy flavor goes so well with the fresh rosemary.

Makes 4 servings

1 lb. pork tenderloin, cut into 8 slices
1 T. butter
1 c. sliced mushrooms
2 T. onion, finely chopped
1 clove garlic, minced
1 t. fresh rosemary, chopped
1/4 t. celery salt
1 T. sherry or apple juice

Flatten each pork slice to one-inch thick; set aside. Melt butter in a large cast-iron skillet over medium-high heat. Cook pork slices just until golden, about one minute per side. Remove pork slices to a plate, reserving drippings in skillet. Add remaining ingredients except sherry or apple juice to skillet. Reduce heat to low; cook for 2 minutes, stirring frequently. Stir in sherry or juice. Return pork slices to skillet; spoon mushroom mixture over top. Cover and simmer for 3 to 4 minutes, until the pork juices run clear. Serve pork slices topped with mushroom mixture.

Rosemary Pork & Mushrooms

Brenda Rogers, Atwood, CA

South-of-the-Border Squash Skillet

Our family grows lots of yellow summer squash in our community garden. We love tacos, so this taco-flavored recipe is a yummy way to use it up! If you omit the meat, it's also a great vegetarian dish.

Makes 4 servings

1 lb. ground beef or turkey
1/3 c. onion, diced
1 c. water
1-1/4 oz. pkg. taco seasoning mix
4 to 5 yellow squash, zucchini or
    crookneck squash, chopped
1 c. shredded Cheddar cheese

In a cast-iron skillet over medium heat, brown meat with onion; drain. Stir in water and taco seasoning; add squash. Cover and simmer for about 10 minutes, until squash is tender. Stir in cheese; cover and let stand just until cheese melts.

FLAVOR BOOST
For a change of pace and a little extra spice, use seasoned ground pork sausage instead of beef or turkey in this skillet recipe. You'll love it!

Roberta Goll, Chesterfield, MI

Roberta's Pepper Steak

This beef dish is as beautiful as it is yummy. I like to serve it right from the cast-iron skillet that I cook it in. Everyone always comments on it and wants the recipe!

Makes 8 servings

1-1/4 lbs. beef round steak, sliced
    into 1/2-inch strips
2 t. canola oil
2 cloves garlic, pressed and divided
2 green and/or red peppers, cut into
    thin strips
2 onions, coarsely chopped
8-oz. pkg. sliced mushrooms
1/2 t. salt
1/2 t. pepper
1 c. beef broth

In a cast-iron skillet over medium heat, brown steak strips with oil and half the garlic. Add peppers and onions; cook until tender. Stir in mushrooms, salt pepper and remaining garlic. Stir in beef broth. Reduce heat to low and simmer for one hour. Add a little water if needed.

Roberta's Pepper Steak

Wendy Jacobs, Idaho Falls, ID.

Ramen Skillet Supper

This is one of my go-to meals for dinners after hectic days of work and school. My daughter Emma loves this dish, and I love making it because it's so simple.

Serves 4

1 lb. ground beef
2-1/2 c. water
2 3-oz. pkgs. beef-flavor ramen
    noodles with seasoning packets
1/2 c. stir-fry sauce
3 c. frozen stir-fry vegetables

Brown beef in a cast-iron skillet over medium heat; drain. Add water, one soup seasoning packet, sauce and vegetables; bring to a boil. Reduce heat to medium-low; cover and cook, stirring occasionally, for 5 minutes, or until vegetables are crisp-tender. Break up noodles; add to skillet. Cover and cook, stirring occasionally, 5 to 8 minutes, until sauce is thickened and noodles are tender.

Cheryl Brady, Canfield, OH

Sweet & Tangy Pork

This is one of our favorite dinners. I usually make brown rice and a veggie to serve with it. It is so easy to make and cookes so quickly. The cast-iron skillet gives it such a nice golden char that tastes so good!

Makes 4 servings

1 t. oil
4 4-oz. boneless pork chops
1/2 c. plus 2 T. tomato soup
2 T. vinegar
1 T. Worcestershire sauce
1 t. brown sugar, packed
8-oz. can pineapple tidbits in own
    juice, drained and 1/4 c. juice
    reserved

Heat oil in a cast-iron skillet over medium heat. Add pork chops and cook until golden on both sides; drain. Stir in soup, vinegar, Worcestershire sauce, brown sugar, pineapple and reserved juice. Cover and simmer over low heat for 5 to 10 minutes until pork is cooked through.

Sweet & Tangy Pork

Doris Stegner, Delaware, OH

Sunday Meatball Skillet

Oh-so delicious alongside roasted green beans.

Serves 4

8-oz. pkg. medium egg noodles, uncooked
3/4 lb. ground beef
1 c. onion, grated
1/2 c. Italian-flavored dried bread crumbs
1 egg, beaten
1/4 c. catsup
1/4 t. pepper
2 c. beef broth
1/4 c. all-purpose flour
1/2 c. sour cream
Garnish: chopped fresh parsley

Cook noodles according to package directions; drain and set aside. Meanwhile, combine beef, onion, bread crumbs, egg, catsup and pepper in a large bowl. Mix well and shape into one-inch meatballs. Spray a cast-iron skillet with non-stick vegetable spray. Cook meatballs over medium heat, turning occasionally, until browned, about 10 minutes. Remove meatballs and let drain

on paper towels. In a bowl, whisk together broth and flour; add to drippings in skillet. Cook and stir until mixture thickens, about 5 minutes. Stir in sour cream. Add cooked noodles and meatballs; toss to coat. Cook and stir until heated through, about 5 minutes. Garnish with parsley.

Carol Hickman, Kingsport, TN

Salmon Patties

A delicious standby...so quick to fix, and most of the ingredients are right in the pantry.

Makes 8 servings

15-1/2 oz. can salmon, drained and flaked
1/4 c. whole-wheat crackers, crushed
1/2 T. dried parsley
1/2 t. lemon zest
1 T. lemon juice
2 green onions, sliced
1 egg plus 1 egg white, beaten
1 T. canola oil

Combine all ingredients except oil; form into 6 patties. Heat oil in cast-iron skillet over medium heat. Cook patties 4 to 5 minutes on each side, until golden. Serve with one tablespoon Cucumber Sauce per serving.

Cucumber Sauce:

1/3 c. cucumber, chopped
3 T. plain yogurt
2 T. mayonnaise
1/4 t. dried tarragon

Combine all ingredients; chill until ready to serve.

Salmon Patties

Kathy Harris, Valley Center, KS

Super-Simple Swiss Steak

This is one of the easiest ways to make Swiss Steak...and it's so delicious.

Serves 6

1 lb. beef round steak, sliced into
   6 pieces
1 t. garlic powder
salt and pepper to taste
1/4 c. all-purpose flour
1/3 c. oil
2 cloves garlic, crushed
1 onion, sliced
1 green pepper, sliced
14-1/2 oz. can diced tomatoes
1-1/4 c. water

Season steak on all sides with garlic powder, salt and pepper. Place flour in a shallow bowl; dredge steak in flour until evenly coated. Heat oil in a Dutch oven over medium heat. Cook steak until browned on all sides. Reduce heat to low; add remaining ingredients. Cook, covered, for 1-½ hours, or until steak is tender and cooked through, adding more water to cover steak if needed.

Wendy Lee Paffenroth, Pine Island, NY

Mom's Beef Stroganoff

So rich and creamy, I love to serve it on Christmas Eve. It is always a hit!

Serves 4

1/2 c. all-purpose flour
1 t. paprika
1 t. dry mustard
1 t. salt
1/2 t. pepper
1-1/2 lbs. stew beef, sliced into strips
2 T. olive oil
1 onion, thinly sliced
3/4 lb. sliced mushrooms
1 c. water
14-1/2 oz. can beef broth
1/2 c. sour cream
8-oz. pkg. wide egg noodles, cooked
Garnish: paprika, dried parsley

Combine flour and seasonings in a large plastic zipping bag. Add beef; seal and shake until all the meat is coated. Remove meat; reserve flour in plastic zipping bag. Heat oil in a Dutch oven over medium heat; brown meat on all sides. Add onion and mushrooms; sauté. Sprinkle with reserved flour; stir to mix. Add water and broth; stir. Reduce heat; cook for about one hour, until sauce is thickened and meat is tender. Remove from heat; stir in sour cream. Do not boil. Place noodles in large serving dish; spoon meat mixture over noodles. Sprinkle with paprika and parsley if desired.

Mom's Beef Stroganoff

Karen Thomas, Princess Anne, MD

Maryland Crab Cakes

A true Maryland summer treat...top with a dollop of mayonnaise if you like. Crab cakes make scrumptious sandwiches or salad toppings too.

Serves 8

1 lb. crabmeat, flaked
3 T. mayonnaise
1 c. saltine crackers, crushed
1 t. seafood seasoning or pepper
1 t. mustard
2 t. Worcestershire sauce
1 egg, beaten
oil for frying

Mix together all ingredients except oil; form into 8 patties. Heat 1/8 inch of oil in a cast-iron skillet over medium heat. Fry patties in oil until golden on both sides. Drain on paper towels.

Kathleen Neff, Claxton, GA

Savory Shrimp & Pasta Toss

The red pepper flakes in this recipe give it just a little heat that makes it extra special!

Serves 4

12-oz. pkg. penne pasta, divided
2 t. olive oil
1 onion, chopped
1 c. fresh tomatoes, diced
1/4 t. red pepper flakes
1/4 t. dried oregano
1 lb. uncooked medium shrimp, peeled and cleaned
1/4 c. fresh parsley, chopped
4-oz. pkg. crumbled feta cheese, divided

Measure out half the package of pasta, reserving the rest for another recipe. Cook as package directs; drain. Meanwhile, in a cast-iron skillet, heat oil over medium heat. Add onion; cook until tender and lightly golden. Stir in tomatoes and their juice, red pepper flakes and oregano; cook until boiling over high heat. Reduce heat to medium; cook sauce until slightly thickened, stirring occasionally. Stir in shrimp; cook for 2 to 4 minutes, until pink. Remove skillet from heat; stir in parsley and 1/2 cup feta cheese. Add cooked pasta to skillet mixture and toss to coat. Use remaining cheese to top each serving.

Savory Shrimp & Pasta Toss

Doris Garner, Los Angeles, CA

Cornmeal Fried Catfish & Fresh Tartar Sauce

Serve these easy-to-prepare fillets with homemade tartar sauce or your favorite bottled cocktail sauce.

Serves 6

3 large or 6 small catfish fillets
1/2 c. mustard
1 c. cornmeal
1 t. salt
1/2 t. pepper
2 T. oil
Garnish: lemon wedges

Rinse and dry fillets; brush with mustard. Combine cornmeal, salt and pepper in a large plastic zipping bag; shake bag to mix well. Pour oil into a cast-iron skillet and place over medium-high heat. Add one fillet to bag and shake to coat; add fillet to skillet, fry until golden on both sides and place in a brown paper bag to keep crisp. Repeat with remaining fillets, adding more oil, if needed. Serve with lemon wedges and Fresh Tartar Sauce.

Fresh Tartar Sauce:
1/2 c. sour cream
1/2 c. mayonnaise
1 t. lemon juice
2 T. onion, diced
1 T. fresh parsley, chopped

Combine all ingredients in a small bowl and mix well. Cover and refrigerate until chilled. Makes 1-1/4 cups.

Gail Blain, Grand Island, NE

Ham Steak & Apples Skillet

My grandmother's old black cast-iron skillet brings back wonderful memories of the delicious things she used to make in it. I seek out scrumptious skillet recipes just so I can use Grandma's old skillet...this one is a real family favorite.

Serves 6

3 T. butter
1/2 c. brown sugar, packed
1 T. Dijon mustard
2 c. apples, cored and diced
2 1-lb. bone-in ham steaks

Melt butter in a cast-iron skillet over medium heat. Add brown sugar and mustard; bring to a simmer. Add apples; cover and simmer for about 5 minutes. Top apples with ham steaks. Cover with a lid; simmer for 10 more minutes or until apples are tender. Remove ham to a platter and cut into serving-size pieces. Top ham with apples and sauce.

Ham Steak & Apples Skillet

Kathy Dassel, Newburgh, TN

Savory Rice Casserole

A delicious and super-easy dish. It can bake alongside chicken or pork chops.

Serves 6 to 8

8-oz. can sliced water chestnuts, drained and liquid reserved
4-oz. can sliced mushrooms, drained and liquid reserved
1/2 c. butter, sliced
1 c. long-cooking rice, uncooked
10-1/2 oz. can French onion soup

In a cast-iron skillet over medium heat, sauté water chestnuts and mushrooms in butter. Add uncooked rice, soup and reserved liquids. Cover skillet tightly; transfer to oven. Bake at 375 degrees for 45 to 60 minutes, until rice is tender.

DID YOU KNOW?
Heavy-duty cookware made of cast iron is valued for its ability to maintain high temperatures for a long period of time.

Sarah Jose, Shreveport, LA

One-Pot Beef Ravioli

This recipe is the perfect solution for a busy weeknight. I can have this on the table in less than 30 minutes, and there's only one pot to wash!

Serves 4

1 lb. lean ground beef
1 t. oil
1 onion, diced
8-oz. pkg. sliced mushrooms
2 cloves garlic, minced
2 26-oz. jars tomato-basil pasta sauce
1 c. water
1 T. Italian seasoning
1/2 t. salt
1/4 t. pepper
20-oz. pkg. refrigerated 4-cheese ravioli, uncooked
1 c. shredded mozzarella cheese

Brown beef in a Dutch oven over medium-high heat; drain and set beef aside in a bowl. Add oil to Dutch oven; sauté onion and mushrooms for 8 minutes, or until tender. Add garlic and cook for one minute. Stir in beef, pasta sauce, water and seasonings; bring to a boil. Add ravioli to sauce; reduce heat to medium-low. Cover and simmer, stirring occasionally, for 8 to 10 minutes, until pasta is cooked. Stir in cheese.

One-Pot Beef Ravioli

Suzanne Rutan, Auburn, NY

Black-Eyed Peas & Potato Skillet

Nothing beats the taste of freshly snipped dill from your herb garden... so zesty and bright!

Serves 2

1/3 c. dried black-eyed peas
1-1/2 c. new redskin potatoes, halved
1 T. olive oil
1 red onion, diced
1 T. fresh rosemary, chopped
2 T. fresh dill, chopped
1/4 t. salt
2 eggs
Garnish: chopped fresh dill

Fill a large saucepan with water; bring to a boil. Add peas and cook until almost tender, about 15 to 18 minutes. Add potatoes and cook another 5 to 6 minutes, until potatoes and peas are tender. Drain and set aside. Heat oil in a large cast-iron skillet over medium heat. Add onion and cook until translucent, about 4 to 5 minutes. Stir in potatoes, peas and seasonings. Cook until potatoes are golden. Make 2 wells in potato mixture and crack one egg into each well. Cover and cook until eggs reach desired doneness. Remove from heat and sprinkle with dill.

Julie Swenson, Minneapolis, MN

Spicy Pork Noodle Bowls

So colorful and so tasty. We make these often.

Serves 4

8-oz. pkg. linguine pasta, uncooked
    and divided
2 T. oil, divided
1 lb. boneless pork shoulder, sliced
    into strips
1 onion, thinly sliced
1/2 lb. broccoli, cut into bite-size
    flowerets
2 T. Worcestershire sauce
1 T. soy sauce
2 t. cornstarch
1/2 t. curry powder
1 tomato, chopped

Cook half of pasta according to package directions; set aside. Reserve remaining pasta for another recipe. Heat one tablespoon oil in a large cast-iron skillet over high heat. Add pork; cook and stir until golden, about 7 minutes. Remove pork; set aside. Heat remaining oil in skillet; add onion and broccoli. Cook and stir until tender, about 5 minutes. Mix together sauces, cornstarch and curry powder in a cup; stir into skillet. Cook and stir until slightly thickened. Return pork to pan; heat through. Divide cooked pasta into 4 shallow bowls. Top with pork mixture and tomato; toss to coat pasta.

Spicy Pork Noodle Bowls

Christy Young, North Attleboro, MA

Bowties, Sausage & Beans

This is a hearty and delicious meal anytime...stellar served with a side salad and thick slices of Italian bread.

Serves 6

1 T. olive oil
6 hot Italian pork sausage links,
   sliced into thirds
1 tomato, chopped
2 15-oz. cans cannellini beans
10-oz. pkg. fresh spinach
garlic powder and dried basil to taste
12-oz. pkg. bowtie pasta, cooked

Heat oil in a Dutch oven over medium heat. Cook sausage until browned on all sides and no longer pink in the center; stir in tomato. Simmer, stirring occasionally, until tomato is soft. Stir in beans and seasonings; heat through. Fold in spinach. Cover and simmer until spinach is wilted, about 6 to 8 minutes. Stir in pasta; toss to mix and heat through.

Cecillia Olliveres, Santa Paula, CA

Curried Chicken with Mango

I love dishes like this one that don't take too long to make and have a unique flavor. This recipe is delicious and speedy...perfect served with a side of naan flatbread.

Serves 4 to 6

2 T. oil
4 boneless, skinless chicken breasts,
   cooked and sliced
13.6-oz. can coconut milk
1 c. mango, peeled, pitted and cubed
2 to 3 T. curry powder
cooked jasmine rice

Heat oil in a large cast-iron skillet over medium heat. Cook chicken in oil until golden and warmed through. Stir in milk, mango and curry powder. Simmer for 10 minutes, stirring occasionally, or until slightly thickened. Serve over cooked rice.

Curried Chicken with Mango

Tina Vogel, Orlando, FL

Lucky-7 Mac & Cheese

Wow! This homestyle favorite has seven kinds of cheese...sure to be the cheesiest, tastiest mac & cheese you've ever had.

Makes 6 to 8 servings

16-oz. pkg. elbow macaroni,
    uncooked
1 c. milk
1/2 c. extra-sharp Cheddar cheese,
    diced
1/2 c. Colby cheese, diced
1/2 c. pasteurized process cheese
    spread, diced
1/2 c. Swiss cheese, diced
1/2 c. provolone cheese, diced
1/2 c. Monterey Jack cheese, diced
1/2 c. crumbled blue cheese
salt and pepper to taste

Cook macaroni according to package directions; drain. Meanwhile, in a cast-iron Dutch oven, combine milk and cheeses. Cook over medium-low heat until melted, stirring often. Fold in cooked macaroni until coated well; season with salt and pepper. Heat through over low heat, stirring occasionally.

Barbara Rannazzisi, Gainesville, VA

Mom's Sicilian Pot Roast

Rotini pasta adds to the Sicilian twist of this pot roast...as do the other Italian flavors. It would be just as yummy served over hot cooked rice or savory mashed potatoes.

Serves 8 to 10

4-lb. rolled rump beef roast
2 T. garlic-flavored olive oil
2 28-oz. cans whole tomatoes
2 8-oz. cans Italian tomato sauce
1/2 c. water
1 T. garlic, minced
1 t. dried oregano
1 t. dried basil
1 t. dried parsley
1-1/2 t. salt
1/2 t. pepper
Optional: 1/4 c. all-purpose flour,
    2 c. hot water
hot cooked rotini pasta
Garnish: fresh oregano sprigs

Brown roast slowly in oil over medium heat in a Dutch oven. Add tomatoes with juice, tomato sauce, water, garlic and seasonings. Bring to a boil; cover, reduce heat and simmer 2-1/2 hours or until tender, turning occasionally. Cut roast into serving-size slices. Return meat to Dutch oven; simmer, uncovered, 30 more minutes. If sauce is not thick enough, combine flour and water, stirring until dissolved. Gradually stir flour mixture into sauce, a little at a time, until sauce thickens. To serve, place prepared pasta on a large platter; top with sauce and sliced meat. Garnish with fresh oregano sprigs.

Mom's Sicilian Pot Roast

Angela Lengacher, Montgomery, IN

Fluffy Chicken & Dumplings

This is a wonderful way to warm up on a chilly night! Soft, fluffy dumplings in a warm and hearty mixture of chicken and vegetables... pure comfort food.

Serves 6

1 to 2 T. oil
1 c. celery, chopped
1 c. carrots, peeled and sliced
1 T. onion, chopped
49-oz. can chicken broth
10-3/4-oz. can cream of chicken soup
1/8 t. pepper
2 c. cooked chicken, cubed
1-2/3 c. biscuit baking mix
2/3 c. milk

Heat oil in a Dutch oven over medium-high heat. Sauté celery, carrots and onion in oil for about 7 minutes, until crisp-tender. Add broth, soup and pepper; bring to a boil. Reduce heat to low; stir in chicken and bring to a simmer. In a separate bowl, stir together baking mix and milk. Drop batter by tablespoonfuls into simmering broth. Cover and cook over low heat for 15 minutes without lifting lid. Serve immediately.

Lauren Vanden Berg, Grandville, MI

Skillet Meatloaf

My great-grandma was very poor and only owned one cast-iron skillet. She made this meatloaf in the skillet. She passed her skillet on to my grandma, who passed it on to me. Now this is the only kind of meatloaf I make.

Serves 3 to 4

1 lb. ground beef
1 onion, chopped
1 green pepper, chopped
4 saltine crackers, crushed
1-oz. pkg. ranch salad dressing mix
1 egg
1/4 c. barbecue sauce

In a bowl, combine beef, onion and green pepper; mix well. Add cracker crumbs and dressing mix; mix again. Shape beef mixture into ball; make a little hole in the middle. Crack the egg into the hole; mix again. Shape meatloaf to fit in cast-iron skillet(s). Add meatloaf to skillet(s). Spread barbecue sauce on top. Bake at 350 degrees for 30 to 35 minutes for a large skillet and about 20 to 25 minutes for smaller skillets, until meatloaf is no longer pink in the center. Use a meat thermometer to check temperature if desired.

Skillet Meatloaf

Jill Ross, Pickerington, OH

Kale & Potato Casserole

Warm potatoes, wilted greens and Parmesan cheese makes this a favorite vegetarian main dish meal.

Serves 4 to 6

1/4 c. butter, melted
3 potatoes, thinly sliced
10 leaves fresh kale, finely chopped
5 T. grated Parmesan cheese
salt and pepper to taste

Drizzle melted butter over potatoes in a bowl; mix well. In a greased cast-iron skillet layer 1/3 each of potatoes, kale and Parmesan cheese; season with salt and pepper. Continue layering and seasoning, ending with cheese. Cover skillet and transfer to oven. Bake at 375 degrees for 30 minutes. Uncover; bake for another 15 to 30 minutes, until potatoes are tender.

Maryann McGonigle, Greensburg, PA

Birdie's Summer Spaghetti

Whether you choose to use traditional pasta or spiralized summer squash, this dish will be your go-to summer meal.

Makes 6 servings

1 T. canola oil
2 cloves garlic, minced
3 tomatoes, diced
1/4 c. fresh basil, sliced
8-oz. pkg. whole-wheat angel hair pasta, cooked or 2 yellow summer squash, peeled and spiralized
1 t. butter
1/4 t. salt
1/2 t. pepper
1/4 c. flat-leaf parsley, chopped
Garnish: grated Parmesan cheese

Add oil to a cast-iron skillet over medium heat. Stir in garlic and cook about 30 seconds. Add tomatoes; stir and sauté until tomatoes become juicy. Add basil and cook for 3 to 4 minutes. Transfer pasta to a serving bowl; toss with butter, salt, pepper and parsley. Top with tomato mixture. Garnish with cheese; toss to coat.

Birdie's Summer Spaghetti

Emma Brown, Ontario, Canada

Southwestern Corn Skillet

This is one of the easiest dishes I make. All the hearty southwestern flavors and gooey cheese...definitely a stick-to-your-ribs meal.

Serve 6

1 lb. ground beef
1/2 c. onion, chopped
26-oz. jar pasta sauce
11-oz. can sweet corn & diced
   peppers
1/2 t. salt
8-oz. pkg rotini pasta, cooked
1 c. shredded Cheddar cheese
4 green onions, sliced

Brown beef and onion in a cast-iron skillet over medium heat; drain. Stir in pasta sauce, corn, salt and pasta. Cook and stir until heated through. Remove from heat and sprinkle with cheese. Cover and let stand until cheese is melted; sprinkle with green onions.

Jo Ann, Gooseberry Patch

Picture-Perfect Paella

This classic Spanish dish is not only beautiful to look at, it's also amazingly delicious. It takes a little time to prepare, but it's so worth it.

Serves 8

3 lbs. chicken
2 onions, quartered
1 stalk celery, sliced
2 carrots, peeled and sliced
salt and pepper to taste
6 c. water
2 c. long-cooking rice, uncooked
2 cloves garlic, crushed
1/4 c. oil
1 c. peas
1/4 c. diced pimentos, drained
1/2 t. dried oregano
1/8 t. saffron or turmeric
1 lb. uncooked large shrimp, peeled
   and cleaned
12 uncooked clams in shells

In a large cast-iron skillet over medium heat, combine chicken pieces, onions, celery, carrots, salt, pepper and water. Bring to a boil; reduce heat, cover and simmer for one hour. Remove vegetables and chicken, reserving 6 cups broth. Dice chicken and set meat aside, discarding bones. In the same skillet over medium heat, cook and stir rice and garlic in oil until golden. Add reserved chicken, reserved broth, peas, pimentos, oregano and saffron or turmeric. Cover and cook over low heat for 15 minutes. Add shrimp and clams; cover and cook for another 10 minutes, or until shrimp are pink and clams have opened.

Picture-Perfect Paella

Amy Holt, Enterprise, UT

Tempting Teriyaki Chicken

I have to triple this recipe when I make it for my family...they absolutely love it.

Serves 4 to 6

2/3 c. soy sauce
1/3 c. sugar
1/4 t. ground ginger
1/8 t. garlic powder
4 to 5 boneless, skinless chicken
    breasts
cooked rice
Garnish: sliced green onions,
    sesame seed

In a large cast-iron skillet over medium heat, whisk together soy sauce, sugar, ginger and garlic powder. When heated through, add chicken. Cover and simmer, basting chicken occasionally with sauce, for about 30 minutes, until chicken is no longer pink in the center. Uncover and cook an additional 10 minutes, or until sauce thickens. Serve with rice; garnish with green onions and sesame seed.

Anita Mullins, Eldridge, MO

Anita's Onion Steaks

A simply delicious way to fix budget-friendly cube steaks! Serve them with mashed potatoes, cooked egg noodles or rice, with the gravy from the skillet ladled over all.

Serves 4

15-oz. can beef broth
1.35-oz. pkg. onion soup mix
1 onion, thinly sliced
4 beef cube steaks
pepper to taste
10-3/4 oz. can cream of onion soup

In a cast-iron skillet over medium heat, combine broth and soup mix; mix well. Add onion and steaks; sprinkle with pepper to taste. Reduce heat to low; cover and simmer for 30 minutes. Turn steaks over; cover and simmer for an additional 30 minutes. Remove steaks to a plate; stir soup into mixture in skillet. Return steaks to skillet, being sure to coat each steak with gravy. Cover and simmer over low heat for 15 minutes.

Aimee Bowlin, Keithville, LA

Creamy Chicken Spaghetti

This is one of my husband's favorite meals, and I enjoy making it because it's so quick & easy.

Serves 8

2 lbs. chicken breasts, cooked and
    shredded
16-oz. pkg. spaghetti, cooked
2 14-1/2 oz. cans stewed tomatoes,
    chopped
2 10-3/4 oz. cans cream of chicken soup
10-3/4 oz. can cream of mushroom soup
8-oz. pkg. pasteurized process cheese
    spread, cubed
4-oz. can mushrooms, drained

Combine all ingredients in a Dutch oven; cook over medium heat until warmed through and cheese is melted.

Creamy Chicken Spaghetti

Gail Blain, Grand Island, NE

Skillet BBQ Chicken

A family favorite that uses pantry staples and my beloved cast-iron skillet. I love that it all goes into one skillet and doesn't require a lot of prep. Perfect for busy-night suppers!

Serves 4.

2 to 3 T. olive oil
4 chicken breasts, boneless or
    bone-in
1 onion, sliced
2/3 c. catsup
2/3 c. water
3 T. red wine vinegar
3 T. brown sugar, packed
1 T. Worcestershire sauce
1 t. chili powder
1/2 t. dry mustard
1/2 t. celery seed
Optional: chopped fresh parsley

In a large cast-iron skillet, heat oil over medium-high heat. Brown chicken on both sides; remove to a plate. Add onion to skillet; sauté until tender. Stir in remaining ingredients except garnish; bring to a boil. Return chicken to skillet, skin-side down. Reduce heat to medium-low; cover and cook for 30 minutes. Turn chicken over; cover and simmer an additional 20 minutes, or until chicken juices run clear when pierced. To serve, spoon sauce from skillet over chicken. Garnish with parsley, if desired.

Tami Bowman, Marysville, OH

Speedy Skillet Lasagna

This dish is so quick to make...you don't even have to cook the pasta before you assemble it!

Serves 4 to 5

1 lb. ground turkey
1/4 t. garlic powder
1/4 t. Italian seasoning
2 14-oz. cans beef broth with onion
14-1/2 oz. can diced tomatoes
2 c. rotini pasta, uncooked
1/2 c. shredded mozzarella cheese
Garnish: 1/4 c. grated Parmesan
    cheese

In a cast-iron skillet over medium heat, brown ground turkey; drain and add seasonings. Stir in broth and tomatoes with juice; heat to boiling. Add rotini. Cover skillet; cook over medium heat for 10 minutes. Uncover and cook another 5 to 10 minutes until rotini is tender. Stir in mozzarella cheese; top each serving with Parmesan cheese.

Speedy Skillet Lasagna

Stephanie Whisenhunt,
Birmingham, AL

Easy Spaghetti & Meatballs

One taste of this homemade sauce, and family & friends will think that it has simmered all day long. You don't have to share that it only took 20 minutes to make!

Serves 4 to 6

10-oz. pkg. spaghetti, uncooked
24 frozen, cooked Italian-style
  meatballs, thawed
2 14-oz. cans Italian-style diced
  tomatoes
2 6-oz. cans tomato paste
1/2 c. water
2 t. Italian seasoning
2 t. sugar
Optional: grated Parmesan cheese

Cook pasta according to package directions; keep pasta warm. Meanwhile, add meatballs, undrained tomatoes and next 4 ingredients to a Dutch oven. Cook over medium heat 20 minutes, stirring occasionally. Serve over hot cooked pasta. Sprinkle with Parmesan cheese, if desired.

Sharlene Casteel, Phenix City, AL

Texas Hash

This is my go-to recipe for when we have little time to spare but everyone is hungry! It is quick and easy to make...you'll love this hearty chili-like dish!

Makes 6 servings

1 lb. ground beef
1 onion, diced
1 red or green pepper, diced
1 c. long-cooking brown rice,
  uncooked
14-1/2 oz. can diced tomatoes
2 c. water
2 t. chili powder
1 t. paprika
1/4 t. salt
1/4 t. pepper
Garnish: fresh thyme sprigs

Brown beef with onion and red or green pepper in a cast-iron skillet over medium heat; drain. Stir in uncooked rice and remaining ingredients except garnish. Cover and simmer over low heat 25 minutes, or until water is absorbed and rice is tender. Garnish with fresh thyme sprigs.

Texas Hash

Diane Axtell, Marble Falls, TX

BBQ Pork Ribs

We like to pair these juicy ribs with a big platter of corn on the cob. It is always the favorite meal of the summer!

Serves 4 to 6

3 qts. water
4 lbs. pork ribs, cut into serving-size portions
1 onion, quartered
2 t. salt
1/4 t. pepper

Bring water to a boil in a cast-iron Dutch oven over high heat. Add ribs, onion, salt and pepper. Reduce heat to medium-low. Cover and simmer for 1-1/2 hours, or until ribs are tender, stirring occasionally. Prepare BBQ Sauce while ribs are simmering. Remove ribs to a platter; drain and discard cooking liquid. Grill or broil ribs for 10 minutes on each side, brushing often with BBQ Sauce, until sauce is caramelized.

BBQ Sauce:
1/2 c. brown sugar, packed
1/2 c. vinegar
1/2 c. chili sauce
1/4 c. Worcestershire sauce
2 T. onion, chopped
1 T. lemon juice
1/2 t. dry mustard
1/8 t. garlic powder
1/8 t. cayenne pepper

Combine all ingredients in a small saucepan. Simmer over low heat for 30 minutes, stirring often.

J.J. Presley, Portland, TX

Cheesy Sausage-Potato Casserole

Add some fresh green beans too, if you like.

Serves 6 to 8

3 to 4 potatoes, sliced
2 8-oz. pork links sausage, sliced into 2-inch lengths
1 onion, chopped
1/2 c. butter, sliced
1 c. shredded Cheddar cheese

Layer potatoes, sausage and onion in a cast-iron skillet sprayed with non-stick vegetable spray. Dot with butter; sprinkle with cheese. Bake at 350 degrees for 1-1/2 hours.

Cheesy Sausage-Potato Casserole

Ruth's Swiss Bacon-Onion Dip, p. 220

CHAPTER FOUR

FAVORITE
Sides, Breads & Snacks

Italian Egg Rolls, p. 222

Berry-Picker's Reward Muffins, p. 218

Judy Scherer, Benton, MO

Mississippi Hushpuppies

My dad loved to go fishing. He would make these hushpuppies almost every week when I was growing up. We like them with mustard for dipping.

Serves 4

3/4 c. self-rising cornmeal
1/2 c. self-rising flour
1-1/2 T. baking powder
3 eggs, beaten
1/2 c. onion, diced
1/4 c. buttermilk
oil or bacon drippings for deep
   frying

In a bowl, combine cornmeal, flour, baking powder, eggs and onion. Stir in enough buttermilk to moisten mixture; stir until well mixed. Heat several inches of oil or drippings in a cast-iron skillet over medium-high heat. Drop batter into hot oil by teaspoonfuls. Fry until golden on both sides. Drain; serve warm.

Nancy Wise, Little Rock, AR

Homestyle Green Beans

This is a tasty way to serve fresh green beans.

Serves 8

2 lbs. green beans, trimmed
2 c. water
1-1/4 t. salt, divided
1/3 c. butter
1-1/2 T. sugar
1 t. dried basil
1/2 t. garlic powder
1/4 t. pepper
2 c. cherry or grape tomatoes, halved

Place beans in a Dutch oven; add water and one teaspoon salt. Bring to a boil; cover, reduce heat and simmer 15 minutes or until tender. Drain; keep warm. Melt butter in a saucepan over medium heat; stir in sugar, basil, garlic powder, remaining 1/4 teaspoon salt and pepper. Add tomatoes and cook, stirring gently until heated through. Pour tomato mixture over beans and toss gently. Serve hot.

Homestyle Green Beans

Julie Vidovich, Winston-Salem, NC

Garlicky Parmesan Asparagus

Savor the flavor of garden-fresh asparagus in this simple recipe...nice with a baked ham.

Makes 4 servings

1 T. butter
1/4 c. olive oil
2 cloves garlic, minced
1 lb. asparagus spears, trimmed
2 t. lemon juice
salt and pepper to taste
Garnish: shredded Parmesan cheese

Combine butter and oil in a cast-iron skillet over medium heat. Add garlic and sauté for one to 2 minutes. Add asparagus and cook to desired tenderness, stirring occasionally, about 10 minutes. Drain; sprinkle asparagus with lemon juice, salt and pepper. Arrange on serving platter; sprinkle with Parmesan.

Rachel Anderson, Livermore, CA

Granny's Country Cornbread

Pour the batter into vintage cast-iron cornstick pans...the kids will love 'em!

Makes 4 to 6 servings

1-1/4 c. cornmeal
3/4 c. all-purpose flour
5 T. sugar
2 t. baking powder
1 t. baking soda
1/2 t. salt
1 c. buttermilk
1/3 c. oil
1 egg, beaten
1 c. shredded sharp Cheddar cheese
1 c. corn
1 T. jalapeño pepper, minced

Mix together cornmeal, flour, sugar, baking powder, baking soda and salt in a large bowl. Make a well in center; pour in buttermilk, oil and egg. Stir just until ingredients are lightly moistened. Fold in cheese, corn and jalapeño; pour into a greased 8" cast-iron skillet. Bake at 375 degrees for 20 minutes, or until a tester inserted in the center comes out clean. Let cool slightly; cut into wedges.

FAVORITE SIDES, BREADS & SNACKS

Granny's Country Cornbread

Jenita Davison, La Plata, MO

Crispy Zucchini & Onion

This is my husband's favorite way to use all the zucchini from our garden. It's flavorful and crisp...just the way we like it!

Serves 4

1 egg
2 to 3 T. evaporated milk
1/4 c. cornmeal
1/2 c. all-purpose flour
1 t. seasoned salt
1/2 t. garlic salt
1 t. pepper
1 to 2 zucchini, thinly sliced
3 to 4 T. oil
1 onion, thinly sliced

In a shallow bowl, beat egg and milk. Combine cornmeal, flour and seasonings in a large plastic zipping bag. Add zucchini to egg mixture; stir to coat. Add zucchini to bag; shake well to coat. Heat oil in a cast-iron skillet over medium-high heat. Cook zucchini until crisp on one side. Coat onion in egg and cornmeal mixtures; add to skillet. Continue cooking until tender and crisp on both sides.

Lucy Davis, Colorado Springs, CO

Lucy's Sausage Salad

This deliciously different salad may be made ahead and chilled for one to 2 hours, or served immediately. It is so quick to make!

Serves 4

14-oz. pkg. mini smoked beef
    sausages, divided
1 t. canola oil
1 c. corn
15-1/2 oz. can black beans, drained
    and rinsed
1 T. canned jalapeño pepper, seeded
    and minced
1 c. red pepper, chopped
Garnish: fresh cilantro sprigs

Measure out half the sausages; set aside for a future use. Slice remaining sausages into 3 pieces each. In a cast-iron skillet, sauté sausages in oil over medium heat until lightly golden; drain. In a large bowl, combine corn, beans, jalapeño and red pepper. Stir in sausage. Toss with Dressing; garnish with cilantro.

Dressing:
3 T. plain yogurt
3 T. sour cream
1/4 c. picante sauce
1/2 c. fresh cilantro, chopped
salt and pepper to taste

Whisk together all ingredients.

Lucy's Sausage Salad

Kelly Anderson, Erie, PA

Panzanella Salad

This traditional Italian salad is so delicious...a wonderful way to use veggies fresh from the farmers' market.

Makes 6 to 8 servings

1/2 loaf Italian bread, cubed
1/4 c. olive oil
salt and pepper to taste
1 red pepper, chopped
1 yellow pepper, chopped
1 orange pepper, chopped
1 cucumber, chopped
1 red onion, chopped
1 pt. cherry or grape tomatoes
1 to 2 T. capers, drained
6 leaves fresh basil, cut into long,
    thin strips
3/4 c. Italian salad dressing or
    vinaigrette

In a cast-iron skillet, toss together bread cubes, olive oil, salt and pepper. Cook over medium-high heat, stirring occasionally, until crisp and golden; drain and cool. Combine remaining ingredients in a large salad bowl. Just before serving, add bread cubes; toss to coat.

Debbie Muer, Encino, CA

Potato Latkes

This is one of our favorite recipes to serve during Hanukkah. We make them as a family and look forward to celebrating together. The kids love them with applesauce and the adults seem to prefer the sour cream. No matter what you choose, these are delicious!

Serves 4 to 6

2 c. potatoes, peeled and grated
2 eggs, beaten
1/8 t. baking powder
1-1/2 t. salt
1 T. all-purpose flour or matzo meal
1/8 t. pepper
oil for frying
Garnish: sour cream or applesauce

Mix all ingredients except oil and garnish together. Heat oil in a cast-iron skillet over medium-high heat. Pour about one tablespoon of batter for each pancake into hot oil and fry until golden. Top with a dollop of sour cream or applesauce.

Potato Latkes

Amber Erskine, Hartland, VT

Hot Bacon-Potato Salad

This salad is just right for toting to a family reunion.

Makes 4 to 6 servings

3/4 lb. bacon
3/4 c. celery, sliced
1/2 c. onion, chopped
1-1/2 T. all-purpose flour
3/4 c. water
1/3 c. vinegar
2 T. sugar
1-1/2 t. salt
1 t. mustard
1/4 t. celery seed
4 c. potatoes, peeled, cooked and
    sliced

Cook bacon in a cast-iron skillet over medium heat until crisp. Remove bacon; crumble and set aside. Add celery and onion to drippings in skillet; cook until tender. Add remaining ingredients except potatoes; cook until thickened, stirring constantly. Fold in potatoes and bacon; heat through. Serve warm.

Diane Holland, Galena, IL

Rose's 3-Bean Dish

Everyone loves these beans and asks for the recipe. It was given to me by my sister-in-law many years ago. Add a pound of browned hamburger to this if you like.

Makes 10 servings

1/2 lb. bacon
3/4 c. onions, diced
1/2 c. brown sugar packed
1 T. dry mustard
1/2 t. garlic powder
1/2 t. salt
2 16-oz. cans butter beans, drained
28-oz. can Boston baked beans,
    drained
14-1/2 oz. can lima beans, drained
Garnish: fresh chopped parsley

In a Dutch oven over medium heat, cook bacon until crisp Remove bacon to paper towels; partially drain skillet. Add onions to drippings in skillet; cook until lightly golden. Remove onions with a slotted spoon. Add brown sugar and seasonings to pan; cook and stir until brown sugar dissolves. Return onions and crumbled bacon to skillet; add beans. Stir well and heat through over medium-low heat. Garnish with parsley.

Rose's 3-Bean Dish

Janie Collins, Freeport, PA

Campers' Beans

Sweet and satisfying...almost a meal in itself!

Makes 8 to 10 servings

6 to 8 slices bacon
1 onion, chopped
1/4 c. brown sugar, packed
1/4 c. catsup
2 T. mustard
2 t. vinegar
2   32-oz. cans baked beans
Optional: additional crumbled
   bacon

Cook bacon in a cast-iron Dutch oven over medium-high heat. When partially cooked, add onion. Continue cooking until bacon is crisp. Remove bacon and onion to a paper towel; drain pan. To the same pan, add brown sugar, catsup, mustard and vinegar; simmer over low heat for 15 minutes. Stir in beans with liquid, crumbled bacon and onion. Simmer, uncovered, over medium-low heat for at least 30 minutes, stirring often. If desired, garnish with additional bacon.

Ann Farris, Biscoe, AR

Lemon-Garlic Brussels Sprouts

When you sauté the Brussels sprouts, they turn into little gold nuggets of flavor.

Makes 6 servings

3 T. olive oil
2 lbs. Brussels sprouts, trimmed and
   halved
3 cloves garlic, minced
zest and juice of 1 lemon
sea salt and pepper to taste
3 T. Gruyère cheese, grated

Heat oil in a large cast-iron skillet over medium-high heat. Add Brussels sprouts; sauté for 7 to 8 minutes. Turn sprouts over; sprinkle with garlic. Continue cooking 7 to 8 minutes, until sprouts are golden, caramelized and tender. Reduce heat to low. Add remaining ingredients except cheese; stir to combine. Adjust seasonings, as needed. Top with cheese.

Lemon-Garlic Brussels Sprouts

Phyllis Cowgill, La Porte, IN

Granny's Apple Coffee Cake

I remember my dear mother and great-grandmother making this cake with apples and butternuts picked right off the tree and fresh milk from our cows.

Makes 16 servings

1-1/2 c. all-purpose flour
3/4 c. sugar
2 t. baking powder
1 t. cinnamon
1/4 t. salt
1/2 c. butter, softened
2 eggs, beaten
3/4 c. milk
2-1/4 c. apples, peeled, cored, sliced
   and divided

Combine flour, sugar, baking powder, cinnamon and salt in a bowl; mix well. Blend in butter, eggs and milk; pour half of batter into a greased cast-iron skillet. Arrange half of apples over batter; sprinkle with half of the Topping. Arrange remaining apples over Topping, followed by remaining batter and remaining Topping. Bake at 350 degrees for 40 minutes.

Topping:
1/2 c. brown sugar, packed
3 T. all-purpose flour
1/2 c. chopped walnuts
1-1/2 t. cinnamon
1 T. butter

Combine all ingredients in a bowl; mix well.

Vickie, Gooseberry Patch

Creamy Bacon & Herb Succotash

You'll love this deluxe version of an old harvest-time favorite...I do!

Serves 6

1/4 lb. bacon, chopped
1 onion, diced
10-oz. pkg. frozen lima beans
1/2 c. water
salt and pepper to taste
10-oz. pkg. frozen corn
1/2 c. whipping cream
1-1/2 t. fresh thyme, minced
Garnish: 2 t. fresh chives, snipped

Cook bacon until crisp in a Dutch oven over medium-high heat. Remove bacon, reserving about 2 tablespoons drippings in Dutch oven. Add onion; sauté about 5 minutes, or until tender. Add beans, water, salt and pepper; bring to a boil. Reduce heat; cover and simmer 5 minutes. Stir in corn, whipping cream and thyme; return to a simmer. Cook until vegetables are tender, about 5 minutes. Toss with bacon and chives before serving.

Creamy Bacon & Herb Succotash

Kelly Anderson, Erie, PA

Pan-Fried Corn Fritters

Delicious with campfire chili or a big kettle of ham & beans!

Makes 6 to 8 fritters

1 c. biscuit baking mix
8-3/4 oz. can corn, drained
1 egg, beaten
1/4 c. water
1 to 2 T. bacon drippings or oil
Garnish: butter or maple syrup

Combine biscuit mix, corn, egg and water in a bowl; stir well. Grease a cast-iron griddle with drippings or oil. Drop batter onto griddle by 1/4 cupfuls. Cook over medium-low heat for about 5 minutes on each side, until golden. Serve warm with butter or syrup.

Evelyn Moriarty, Philadelphia, PA

Vegetable Quinoa Patties

This recipe is my own, adapted from one I found online and tweaked. It has become a family favorite, especially in summertime when fresh-picked veggies are available.

Makes 6 patties

3 eggs
1/2 c. shredded part-skim
    mozzarella cheese
1/2 c. cottage cheese
1/4 c. whole-wheat flour
1 carrot, peeled and grated
1 zucchini, grated
3 T. green, red or yellow pepper,
    grated
3 green onions, finely chopped
1/2 t. ground cumin
1/4 t. garlic powder
1/8 t. salt
1/4 t. pepper
2 c. cooked quinoa
1 T. olive oil

Beat eggs in a large bowl; stir in cheeses and flour, blending well. Mix in vegetables. Combine seasonings; sprinkle over vegetable mixture and mix well. Add cooked quinoa; stir together well. Heat olive oil in a cast-iron skillet over medium heat. With a small ladle, drop mixture into skillet, making 6 patties. Flatten lightly with ladle to about 1/4-inch thick. Fry patties for 4 to 5 minutes per side, until golden. Serve each patty with 3 tablespoons Dilled Yogurt Dressing.

Dilled Yogurt Dressing:
1/2 c. plain Greek yogurt
1 cucumber, peeled and diced
3 sprigs fresh dill, snipped, or
    1/2 t. dill weed

Stir together all ingredients in a small bowl.

Vegetable Quinoa Patties

Amanda Johnson, Marysville, OH

Kicked-Up Campfire Beans

A fantastic spicy meatless recipe to enjoy around the campfire or backyard fire pit. Adjust the spice to suit your taste.

Serves 6

32-oz. pkg. dried pinto beans
2 red peppers, finely diced
1 onion, finely diced
5 cloves garlic, minced
2 t. chili powder
2 t. salt
2 t. coarse pepper
1 t. cayenne pepper
1 t. ground cumin
1 T. Worcestershire sauce
Optional: 2 t. hot pepper sauce

Cover beans with water in a Dutch oven. Bring to a boil over high heat; reduce to low. Cover and simmer for 2 hours, adding more water as needed. Add peppers, onion and garlic. Cover; cook for another one to 2 hours, adding water as needed. Stir in seasonings and sauces. Simmer an additional 30 to 40 minutes, until thickened and beans are tender.

Marcia Shaffer, Conneaut Lake, PA

Grandma's Skillet Tomatoes

This recipe is so easy and it's always a hit with the guys!

Serves 6

1/4 c. milk
1/2 c. seasoned dry bread crumbs
1 T. green onion, minced
1 T. grated Parmesan cheese
1 t. Italian seasoning
1 t. salt
6 tomatoes, sliced 1/2-inch thick
2 T. olive oil
1/2 c. shredded mozzarella cheese

Place milk in a shallow bowl. In a separate bowl, combine bread crumbs, onion, Parmesan cheese and seasonings; mix well. Dip tomatoes into milk; coat with crumb mixture. Heat oil in a cast-iron skillet over medium-high heat. Cook tomatoes, a few at a time, until golden, about 2 minutes per side. Remove to a plate; sprinkle with mozzarella cheese.

Grandma's Skillet Tomatoes

Laurie Lightfoot, Hawthorne, NV

Fourth of July Beans

It's just not summer without this favorite side dish!

Serves 10 to 12

1 lb. bacon, diced
1 lb. ground beef
1 lb. hot ground pork sausage
1 c. onion, chopped
28-oz. can pork & beans
15-oz. can ranch-style beans
15-oz. can maple-flavored baked
   beans
16-oz. can kidney beans, drained and
   rinsed
1/2 c. barbecue sauce
1/2 c. catsup
1/2 c. brown sugar, packed
1 T. mustard
2 T. molasses
1 t. salt
1/2 t. chili powder

In a large Dutch oven over medium-high heat, cook bacon until crisp; drain, remove and set aside. Cook beef, sausage and onion until meat is browned; drain. Transfer to a greased disposable aluminum roasting pan. Stir in bacon and remaining ingredients; mix well. Cover and bake at 350 degrees for 45 minutes. Uncover and bake for 15 more minutes.

Sherri Cooper, Armada, MI

Skillet-Toasted Corn Salad

Whenever my father comes to visit, he always requests this salad. He usually stops by the local vegetable stand on his way and picks up fresh ears of corn...just for this salad!

Makes 6 to 8 servings

1/3 c. plus 1 T. olive oil, divided
1/3 c. lemon juice
1 T. Worcestershire sauce
3 to 4 dashes hot pepper sauce
3 cloves garlic, minced
1/4 t. salt
1/2 t. pepper
6 ears sweet corn, husked and
   kernels removed
4 red, yellow and/or green peppers,
   coarsely chopped
1/2 c. shredded Parmesan cheese
1 head romaine lettuce, cut
   crosswise into 1-inch pieces

In a jar with a tight-fitting lid, combine 1/3 cup oil, lemon juice, sauces, garlic, salt and pepper. Cover and shake well; set aside. Heat remaining oil in a cast-iron skillet over medium-high heat. Add corn; sauté for 5 minutes, or until corn is tender and golden, stirring often. Remove from heat; keep warm. Combine corn, peppers and cheese in a large bowl. Pour olive oil mixture over top; toss lightly to coat. Serve over lettuce.

Skillet-Toasted Corn Salad

Jody Sinkuta, Dresser, WI

Honeyed Carrots

The sweet taste of these carrots makes this a very popular dish!

Makes 8 servings

5 c. carrots, peeled and sliced
1/4 c. honey
1/4 c. butter, melted
2 T. brown sugar, packed
2 T. fresh parsley, chopped
1/4 t. salt
1/8 t. pepper

Place carrots in a cast-iron skillet; add water to cover. Cook over medium heat just until tender; drain and return to skillet. Combine remaining ingredients in a small bowl and blend well. Pour honey mixture over carrots; toss to coat. Cook over medium heat until carrots are glazed and heated through.

Sonna Johnson, Goldfield, IA

Peppery Peas o' Plenty

Five types of peas, hickory-smoked bacon and drippings, and garlic-chili sauce simmer together for hearty side servings. Serve with warm biscuits or cornbread.

Serves 4 to 6

4 slices bacon
1 onion, chopped
1 c. frozen black-eyed peas
1 c. frozen purple hull peas
1 c. frozen crowder peas
1 c. frozen butter peas
1 c. frozen field peas with snaps
32-oz. container chicken broth
1 T. Asian garlic-chili sauce
3/4 to 1 t. salt
1 T. pepper

Cook bacon in a Dutch oven over medium heat until crisp; remove bacon and drain on paper towels, reserving drippings in pan. Crumble bacon. Sauté onion in reserved drippings over medium-high heat 8 minutes or until translucent. Add remaining ingredients and cook, uncovered, 20 to 25 minutes. Top with crumbled bacon.

Peppery Peas o' Plenty

Stephanie Norton, Saginaw, TX

Company Green Beans

A simple way to jazz up green beans.

Serves 4

3 slices bacon
1/4 c. red onion, finely grated
2 t. garlic, minced
2 14-1/2 oz. cans French-style green
   beans, drained
1 tomato, chopped
salt and pepper to taste
1/2 c. shredded sharp Cheddar
   cheese

Cook bacon in a cast-iron skillet over medium-high heat until crisp. Remove bacon to paper towels, reserving drippings in skillet. Sauté onion and garlic in reserved drippings until slightly softened. Remove from heat; stir in green beans, tomato and seasonings. Sprinkle with cheese. Cover skillet and transfer to oven. Bake at 400 degrees for 15 minutes. Uncover; reduce heat to 350 degrees. Bake an additional 15 minutes, until hot and bubbly.

Vickie, Gooseberry Patch

Sweet Potato Cornbread

This rich cornbread is sure to become your family favorite. Baking in a skillet makes the edges so wonderfully golden. Serve it with honey butter or raspberry jam.

Makes 6 servings

2 c. self-rising cornmeal mix
1/4 c. sugar
1 t. cinnamon
1-1/2 c. milk
1 c. cooked sweet potato, mashed
1/4 c. butter, melted
1 egg, beaten

Whisk together all ingredients just until dry ingredients are moistened. Spoon the batter into a greased cast-iron skillet. Bake at 425 degrees for 30 minutes, or until a toothpick inserted in center comes out clean. Cut into wedges; serve immediately.

Sweet Potato Cornbread

Kathy Grashoff, Fort Wayne, IN

Kathy's Bacon Popovers

Everyone loves bacon! Serve these yummy popovers with a salad for a special dinner.

Makes one dozen

2 eggs, beaten
1 c. milk
1 T. oil
1 c. all-purpose flour
1/2 t. salt
3 slices bacon, crisply cooked and
  crumbled

Whisk together eggs, milk and oil. Beat in flour and salt just until smooth. Fill 12 greased and floured cast-iron muffin cups 2/3 full. Sprinkle bacon evenly over batter. Bake at 400 degrees for 25 to 30 minutes, until puffed and golden. Serve warm.

Kathie Poritz, Burlington, WI

Generations Rhubarb Bread

I've had this recipe for years. Now, I have my grandchildren helping me harvest rhubarb!

Makes 2 loaves

1-1/2 c. rhubarb, finely diced
3/4 c. brown sugar, packed
3/4 c. sugar
1 c. skim milk
1 t. vinegar
2-1/2 c. all-purpose flour
1/2 c. oil
1 egg, beaten
1 t. baking soda
1 t. salt
1 t. vanilla extract
Optional: 1/2 c. chopped nuts
Topping

Sprinkle rhubarb with sugars; set aside. Stir together milk and vinegar. Add remaining ingredients except nuts; stir until thoroughly blended. Stir in rhubarb mixture and nuts, if using. Mix well and pour into 2 greased and floured 9"x5" cast-iron loaf pans. Sprinkle with Topping. Bake at 350 degrees for 50 to 60 minutes, until toothpick tests clean.

Topping:
1/4 c. sugar
1 t. cinnamon
1 T. butter

Mix ingredients with a fork until crumbly.

Generations Rhubarb Bread

Annette Ingram, Grand Rapids, MI

Sassy Squash

My neighbor Jenny is kind enough to share the bounty of her garden. I make sure to keep stewed tomatoes in the pantry when squash are in season!

Serves 6 to 8

1/2 c. red onion, thinly sliced
1 T. butter
3 c. yellow squash, thinly sliced
3 c. zucchini, thinly sliced
1 t. salt
pepper to taste
1 clove garlic, minced
16-oz. can stewed tomatoes

In a cast-iron skillet, sauté onion in butter over medium-high heat for 2 minutes. Stir in remaining ingredients except tomatoes. Reduce heat to medium and cook until crisp-tender. Add tomatoes and cook until heated through.

Susan Pribble-Moore, Roanoke, VA

Low-Fat Chocolate Oat Muffins

The grated zucchini in these muffins makes them so moist and yummy!

Makes one dozen, serves 12

2 c. oat flour
1/3 c. brown sugar, packed
1/3 c. baking cocoa
2 t. baking powder
1/2 t. baking soda
1/2 t. salt
1 c. dark chocolate chips
2/3 c. zucchini, finely grated
1 c. skim milk
1/3 c. honey
2 egg whites, beaten
Garnish: rolled oats

In a bowl, combine flour, brown sugar, baking cocoa, baking powder, baking soda and salt. Mix well; gently stir in chocolate chips. In a separate large bowl, combine remaining ingredients, except garnish; mix well. Add flour mixture to zucchini mixture; stir only until well combined. Spoon batter into a cast-iron muffin pan sprayed with nonstick vegetable spray, filling cups 2/3 full. Sprinkle oats on top of muffins. Bake at 400 degrees for 18 to 20 minutes, until a toothpick tests clean. Cool muffin tin on a wire rack for 10 minutes; remove muffins from tin.

Low-Fat Chocolate Oat Muffins

Mary Patenaude, Griswold, CT

Corn Dog Mini Muffins

These make great party appetizers, or serve with soup or salad for a quick lunch.

Makes about 2-1/2 dozen

8-1/2 oz. pkg. corn muffin mix
1 egg, beaten
1/3 c. milk
1 T. honey mustard
4 hot dogs, cut into 1/2-inch pieces
1/2 c. shredded Cheddar cheese

In a large bowl, stir together muffin mix, egg, milk and mustard. Fold in hot dog pieces and cheese. Drop batter by tablespoonfuls into 32 lightly greased cast-iron mini muffin cups. Bake at 350 degrees for 10 to 15 minutes, until lightly golden. Cool in pan on a wire rack for 5 minutes; turn muffins out of pan.

FLAVOR BOOST
To add a little kick to your muffins, add one tablespoon chopped red or green pepper. Yum!

Diane Widmer, Blue Island, IL

Cranberry-Carrot Loaf

My grandmother gave me this recipe. I've updated it by reducing the sugar, replacing the oil with applesauce and adding cranberries. I think you'll agree it's still packed with old-fashioned goodness!

Makes one loaf, serves 8

2 c. all-purpose flour
3/4 c. sugar
1-1/2 t. baking powder
1-1/2 t. baking soda
1/4 t. salt
1/2 t. cinnamon
1/2 c. carrot, peeled and shredded
1/3 c. light sour cream
1/4 c. unsweetened applesauce
1/4 c. water
2 eggs, lightly beaten
1 c. frozen cranberries

Grease a 9"x5" cast-iron loaf pan; set aside. In a large bowl, mix together flour, sugar, baking powder, baking soda, salt and cinnamon. Stir in carrot to coat. Make a well in center of flour mixture; add sour cream, applesauce, water and eggs. Stir until combined. Slowly stir in cranberries. Spoon batter into pan. Bake on center oven rack at 350 degrees for 60 minutes, or until a toothpick inserted in the center comes out clean. Cool loaf in pan for 15 minutes. Remove to a rack and cool completely.

Cranberry-Carrot Loaf

Jennifer Licon-Conner, Gooseberry Patch

Ultimate Nachos

This is one of our favorite snacks any time of the year.

Serves 6 to 8

1/3 c. onion, finely chopped
1 clove garlic, minced
1 T. olive oil
16-oz. can refried beans
1/2 c. salsa
13-oz. pkg. restaurant-style tortilla
    chips
1-1/2 c. shredded Monterey Jack
    cheese
1-1/2 c. shredded Cheddar cheese
pickled jalapeño slices, well drained
Optional: 1 c. guacamole, 1/2 c. sour
    cream
Optional: chopped fresh cilantro,
    sliced ripe olives, shredded
    lettuce, additional salsa

Sauté onion and garlic in hot oil in a cast-iron skillet over medium heat 4 to 5 minutes or until onion is tender. Add beans and salsa to pan, stirring until beans are creamy. Cook one minute or until heated. Scatter most of chips on a parchment paper-lined large baking sheet or an oven-proof platter. Top with bean mixture, cheeses and desired amount of jalapeños. Bake at 450 degrees for 8 minutes or until cheeses melt and edges are golden. Top with small dollops of guacamole and sour cream, if desired. Add desired toppings. Serve hot.

Jeanne Barringer, Edgewater, FL

Sour Cream Mini Biscuits

This recipe make several dozen bite-size biscuits...ideal for filling gift baskets or taking to a potluck.

Makes 4 dozen

1 c. butter, softened
1 c. sour cream
2 c. self-rising flour

Blend butter and sour cream together until fluffy; gradually mix in flour. Drop teaspoonfuls of dough into a greased mini muffin cast-iron baking tin. Bake at 425 degrees for 10 to 12 minutes.

Sour Cream Mini Biscuits

Tonia Holm, Burlington, ND

Homestyle Spoon Bread

Serve these golden rounds with butter, homemade jam or honey... delicious!

Serves 4

1 c. all-purpose flour
2 t. baking powder
1 t. sugar
1/2 t. salt
oil for deep frying

Mix together all ingredients except oil; blend in 3/4 cup water. Drop dough by tablespoonfuls into a cast-iron skillet filled with 1/4-inch hot oil. Flip dough over when bubbles form along the edges; cook until golden on each side.

Francie Stutzman, Dayton, OH

That Yummy Bread

Homemade bread with a savory herb filling...really unforgettable!

Makes 2 loaves, serves 20

1 c. skim milk
2 T. sugar
1/4 c. butter
2-1/2 t. salt
1 c. water
2 envs. active dry yeast
7 c. all-purpose flour, divided
2 eggs, beaten and divided
1 T. butter, melted

In a medium saucepan, heat milk just to boiling; stir in sugar, butter and salt. Cool to lukewarm and set aside. Heat water until warm (110 to 115 degrees); add yeast, stir to dissolve and add to milk mixture. Pour into a large bowl and add 4 cups flour; stir and beat. Gradually add remaining flour; stir. Let dough rest 10 minutes; turn dough out onto a floured surface and knead until smooth. Place dough in a greased bowl, turning to coat. Cover and let rise in a warm place (85 degrees), away from drafts, until doubled in bulk. Punch down bread dough; shape into 2 balls. Roll out each ball into a 1/4-inch-thick 15"x9" rectangle. Brush with about 2 tablespoons egg, reserving remainder for filling. Spread Herb Filling to one inch from edges of dough; roll up jelly-roll style, starting at short edge. Pinch edges to seal; place in 2 greased 9"x5" cast-iron loaf pans, seam-side down. Brush with butter; cover and let rise in a warm place 55 minutes. Slash tops of loaves with a knife; bake at 375 degrees for one hour. Let cool before slicing.

Herb Filling:
2 c. fresh parsley, chopped
2 c. green onions, chopped
1 clove garlic, minced
2 T. butter
3/4 t. salt
pepper and hot pepper sauce to taste

Sauté parsley, onions and garlic in butter; cool slightly and add reserved egg from bread recipe and remaining ingredients.

That Yummy Bread

Beth Brown, Trent Woods, NC

Hawaiian Asparagus

Serves 4

1 lb. asparagus, trimmed and cut in
    1-inch diagonal slices
2 T. olive oil
1/4 c. beef broth
4 to 5 slices bacon, crisply cooked
    and crumbled
pepper to taste
2 T. toasted sesame seed

In a cast-iron skillet over medium
heat, cook asparagus in oil for 2 to
3 minutes. Add beef broth; reduce
heat to low. Cover and simmer for
4 to 5 minutes, until asparagus is
cooked to desired tenderness. Stir in
crumbled bacon, pepper and sesame
seed.

Vickie, Gooseberry Patch

Cheddar-Dill Corn Muffins

These dressed-up corn muffins are
scrumptious and simple to make.

Makes one dozen

1 c. cornmeal
1 c. all-purpose flour
1/3 c. sugar
2-1/2 t. baking powder
1/2 t. baking soda
1/4 t. salt
1 egg
3/4 c. skim milk
1 c. shredded sharp Cheddar cheese
1 c. corn, thawed if frozen
1/4 c. butter, melted
3 T. fresh dill, minced, or 1 T. dill
    weed

In a large bowl, mix cornmeal, flour,
sugar, baking powder, baking soda
and salt; set aside. In a separate bowl,
whisk together egg and milk; stir
in remaining ingredients. Add egg
mixture to cornmeal mixture; stir
just until moistened. Spoon batter
into a greased cast-iron muffin
pan, filling cups 2/3 full. Bake at
400 degrees for about 20 minutes,
until golden and a toothpick inserted
in the center tests clean. Cool
muffins in tin on a wire rack for
10 minutes before turning out of tin.
Serve warm or at room temperature.

Cheddar-Dill Corn Muffins

Judy Olson, Alberta, Canada

Hot Mushroom Dip

Delicious with crackers, fresh veggies and even cubes of bread.

Makes about 1-1/2 cups

2-1/2 c. mushrooms, chopped
1/2 c. green onions, chopped
3 to 4 T. butter
2 T. all-purpose flour
1/2 t. paprika
1/4 c. milk
1 c. sour cream, divided
1/2 t. salt
1/2 t. pepper
1/8 t. cayenne pepper
assorted snack crackers

In a cast-iron skillet over medium heat, sauté mushrooms and onions in butter until tender. Stir in flour and paprika; add milk and 1/2 cup sour cream. Cook over low heat, stirring occasionally, until bubbly. Stir in remaining sour cream and seasonings. Serve hot with crackers.

DID YOU KNOW?
Once cast iron is hot, it stays hot. So cast-iron pans are great for searing meat.

Lynn Williams, Muncie, IN

Pork & Apple Bites

We love party meatballs, but I was looking for something a little different. These are perfect for a fall tailgating party!

Makes about 3 dozen

1 lb. ground pork
1/4 t. cinnamon
1 t. salt
1/8 t. pepper
1/2 c. Granny Smith apple, peeled, cored and grated
1/4 c. soft rye bread crumbs
1/4 c. chopped walnuts
1/2 c. water
1/2 c. apple jelly

In a large bowl, combine pork and seasonings; mix well. Add apple, bread crumbs and walnuts; mix gently until well blended. Form mixture into balls by tablespoonfuls. Working in batches, brown meatballs in a cast-iron large skillet over medium heat. Drain; return all meatballs to skillet. Pour water into skillet; cover tightly. Cook over medium-low heat for 15 minutes, or until meatballs are no longer pink in the center. Remove meatballs to a serving bowl; cover and set aside. Stir apple jelly into drippings in skillet; cook and stir until jelly is melted. Spoon sauce over meatballs.

Pork & Apple Bites

Carolen Collins, Kansas City, MO

Savory Cheese & Bacon Potatoes

These cheesy mashed potatoes are out of this world!

Makes 8 servings

2-1/2 lbs. Yukon Gold potatoes,
   peeled and quartered
3 T. butter, softened
2-1/2 c. mixed shredded cheeses,
   such as Swiss, Italian and
   casserole style
1/2 to 3/4 c. milk, warmed
4 slices bacon, crisply cooked and
   crumbled
2 t. dried sage
salt and pepper to taste
Optional: additional shredded
   cheese

Cover potatoes with water in a cast-iron Dutch oven. Bring to a boil; cook until tender, 15 to 18 minutes. Drain potatoes; return to warm pan and mash. Blend in butter and cheeses; add enough milk to make a creamy consistency. Stir in crumbled bacon and seasonings. Sprinkle with additional cheese, if desired.

Meri Herbert, Cheboygan, MI

Carroty Bran Muffins

These muffins are filled with all kinds of goodness for your family. Your entire family will love them and you'll know they are so good for them!

Makes 16 muffins

2-1/2 c. all-purpose flour
2-1/2 c. bran cereal
1-1/2 c. sugar
2-1/2 t. baking soda
1 t. salt
2 c. buttermilk
1/3 c. applesauce
2 eggs, beaten
1-1/2 c. carrots, peeled and shredded
1 green apple, cored and chopped
1 c. sweetened dried cranberries
1/2 c. chopped walnuts
1/4 c. ground flax seed

Mix all ingredients together in a large bowl. Cover and refrigerate batter for up to 2 days, or bake right away. Fill the cups in a greased cast-iron muffin pan 2/3 full. Bake at 375 degrees for 15 to 18 minutes; do not overbake. Muffins will become moister if allowed to stand for awhile.

Carroty Bran Muffins

Paula Smith, Ottawa, IL

Quick & Easy Parmesan Asparagus

From oven to table in only 15 minutes!

Serves 8 to 10

4 lbs. asparagus, trimmed
1/4 c. butter, melted
2 c. shredded Parmesan cheese
1 t. salt
1/2 t. pepper

Place asparagus and one inch of water in a large cast-iron skillet. Bring to a boil. Reduce heat; cover and simmer 5 to 7 minutes, until crisp-tender. Drain. Drizzle with butter; sprinkle with Parmesan cheese, salt and pepper. Bake, uncovered, at 350 degrees for 10 to 15 minutes, until cheese is melted.

FLAVOR BOOST
Add crumbled bacon to the top of the asparagus before baking for extra flavor and crunch.

Chad Rutan, Columbus, OH

Sesame Skillet Bread

Stir up a batch of warm bread for tonight's dinner in a snap!

Serves 8

1-1/3 c. cornmeal
2/3 c. whole-wheat flour
2 t. baking powder
1 t. salt
1/4 c. wheat germ
2 T. sesame seed
1-3/4 c. milk
3 T. oil
1 egg, beaten

In a bowl, stir together cornmeal, flour, baking powder, salt, wheat germ and sesame seed. Add milk, oil and egg; stir until moistened. Spoon batter into a greased cast-iron skillet; transfer to oven. Bake, uncovered, at 400 degrees for 25 to 30 minutes. Cut into wedges; serve warm.

Sesame Skillet Bread

Darlene McAdams, Nampa. ID

Texas Hominy

Great for cookouts...serve right from the skillet! Feel free to mix yellow and white hominy.

Makes 10 servings

6 slices bacon, diced
1 onion, finely diced
1 jalapeño pepper, minced and seeds
   removed
2 cloves garlic, minced
4 15-1/2 oz. cans hominy, drained
salt and pepper to taste
1-1/2 c. shredded Cheddar cheese,
   divided
1-1/2 c. shredded Monterey Jack
   cheese, divided
1/2 c. green onion tops, chopped

Cook bacon in a large cast-iron skillet over medium heat until crisp. Remove bacon to paper towels; reserve drippings in skillet. Sauté onion and jalapeño pepper in reserved drippings until tender. Add garlic; cook one to 2 minutes longer. Stir in hominy, salt and pepper. Remove from heat. Stir in one cup each of Cheddar and Monterey Jack cheeses. Smooth out mixture evenly in skillet. Top with remaining cheeses, crumbled bacon and green onions. Transfer skillet to oven. Bake, uncovered, at 375 degrees for 30 minutes, until hot and bubbly.

Cyndy DeStefano, Mercer, PA

Feta Green Beans

This is such a great side dish. Frozen green beans are so handy, but this dish is especially good with green beans right from the garden!

Makes 10 servings

16-oz. pkg. frozen green beans
2 T. butter
16-oz. pkg. sliced mushrooms
1 onion, finely diced
2 cloves garlic, minced
1/4 t. salt
1/2 t. pepper
4-oz. container crumbled reduced-
   fat feta cheese

Prepare green beans according to package directions; drain. Melt butter in a large cast-iron skillet over medium heat. Add mushrooms, onion, garlic, salt and pepper. Cook 5 to 7 minutes, until heated through. Stir in cheese. Serve immediately.

Feta Green Beans

Gretchen Brown, Forest Grove, OR

Chicken Ranch Quesadillas

For an easy-to-handle snack, slice each quesadilla into 8 mini wedges.

Serves 4

1/2 c. ranch dip
8 8-inch flour tortillas
1 c. shredded Cheddar cheese
1 c. shredded Monterey Jack cheese
10-oz. can chicken, drained
1/3 c. bacon bits
Optional: salsa

Spread 2 tablespoons dip on each of 4 tortillas. Top each with one-quarter of the cheeses, chicken and bacon bits. Top with remaining tortillas. Cook each tortilla stack in a lightly greased cast-iron skillet or griddle over medium-high heat until lightly golden. Turn carefully and cook until cheese is melted. Let stand for 2 minutes; slice into wedges. Serve with salsa, if desired.

Rhonda Johnson, Studio City, CA

Bruschetta with Cranberry Relish

I like to use a whole-grain baguette for this tasty bruschetta...it is always a little more chewy plus it adds more nutrition.

Serves 16

1 to 2 T. olive oil
1 T. butter
1 large whole-grain baguette loaf,
    sliced 1/4-inch thick
1 t. orange zest
1 t. lemon zest
1/2 c. chopped pecans
1/2 c. crumbled blue cheese

Add oil and butter to a cast-iron skillet over medium heat. Fry bread lightly on both sides. Arrange on a broiler pan. Spread with Cranberry Relish. Sprinkle with zests, pecans and blue cheese. Place under broiler just until cheese begins to melt. Serve immediately.

Cranberry Relish:
14-oz. can whole-berry cranberry
    sauce
6-oz. pkg. sweetened dried
    cranberries
1/2 c. sugar
1 t. rum extract
1 c. chopped pecans

Stir all ingredients together.

Bruschetta with Cranberry Relish

Sharon Velenosi, Stanton, CA

Whole-Wheat Soda Bread

This is a wonderfully hearty, coarse-textured bread that's terrific with soups and stews.

Makes one loaf

1 c. all-purpose flour
1 t. baking powder
1 t. baking soda
1/2 t. salt
2 T. sugar
2 c. whole-wheat flour
1-1/2 c. buttermilk
1 T. butter, melted

In a large bowl, combine all-purpose flour, baking powder, baking soda, salt and sugar. Add whole-wheat flour; mix well. Add buttermilk; stir just until moistened. Turn dough onto a floured surface. Knead gently for about 2 minutes, until well mixed and dough is smooth. Form dough into a ball; pat into a circle and place in a lightly greased cast-iron skillet. With a floured knife, mark dough into 4 wedges by cutting halfway through to the bottom. Transfer skillet to oven. Bake, uncovered, at 375 degrees for 30 to 40 minutes, until loaf sounds hollow when tapped. Brush with butter; cool on a wire rack.

Nancy Porter, Fort Wayne, IN

Berry-Picker's Reward Muffins

This recipe works well with blueberries and strawberries too.

Makes one dozen

1/2 c. butter, softened
1 c. sugar
2 eggs, beaten
8-oz. container non-fat plain yogurt
1 t. vanilla extract
2 c. all-purpose flour
1 t. baking powder
1/2 t. baking soda
1/4 t. salt
1 c. raspberries
1/4 c. raspberry jam

With an electric mixer on medium-high speed, beat softened butter for 30 seconds. Add sugar; beat until combined. Blend in eggs, yogurt and vanilla. Use a spoon to stir in dry ingredients until just moistened; fold in berries. Spoon batter into a cast-iron muffin pan, filling 2/3 full. Add one teaspoon of raspberry jam to the center of each muffin. Bake at 400 degrees for 15 to 18 minutes, or until a toothpick tests clean. Cool in pan for 5 minutes; transfer to a wire rack to finish cooling.

Berry-Picker's Reward Muffins

Ellen Folkman, Crystal Beach, FL

Baked Artichoke Squares

Party-perfect...these scrumptious little morsels are sure to go quickly!

Serves 8 to 10

2 6-oz. jars marinated artichoke
   hearts
1/2 c. onion, chopped
1 clove garlic, minced
4 eggs, beaten
1/4 c. dry bread crumbs
1/2 t. fresh Italian parsley, chopped
2 c. shredded Cheddar cheese
salt and pepper to taste

Drain liquid from one jar of artichokes into a cast-iron skillet; drain liquid from remaining jar and discard. Chop all artichokes and set aside. Heat liquid in skillet over medium heat. Sauté onion and garlic until soft; drain. In a bowl, combine eggs, bread crumbs and parsley. Stir in onion mixture, chopped artichokes, cheese, salt and pepper. Pour mixture into a greased 13"x9" baking pan. Bake at 325 degrees for 30 to 35 minutes. Cool; cut into small squares.

Ruth Cooksey, Plainfield, IN

Ruth's Swiss Bacon-Onion Dip

A yummy hot appetizer to serve with your favorite snack crackers.

Makes 4 cups

8 slices bacon
8-oz. pkg. cream cheese, softened
1 c. shredded Swiss cheese
1/2 c. mayonnaise
2 T. green onions, chopped
1 c. round buttery crackers, crushed

In a cast-iron skillet over medium-high heat, cook bacon until crisp. Remove bacon to paper towels. Drain skillet and wipe clean. Mix cheeses, mayonnaise and onion; spread in same skillet. Top with crumbled bacon and cracker crumbs. Transfer skillet to oven. Bake, uncovered, at 350 degrees for 15 to 20 minutes until hot and bubbly.

Ruth's Swiss Bacon-Onion Dip

Carolyn Scilanbro, Hampton, VA

Italian Egg Rolls

These always go fast at our parties... yum!

Makes 8

1/2 c. onion, chopped
1/2 c. green pepper, chopped
2 t. oil
1 lb. ground sweet or hot Italian pork
    sausage
2 10-oz. pkgs. frozen chopped
    spinach, thawed and drained
3 c. shredded mozzarella cheese
1/2 c. grated Parmesan cheese
1/2 t. garlic powder
14-oz. pkg. egg roll wrappers
olive oil for deep frying
Garnish: pizza sauce, warmed

Sauté onion and green pepper in oil in a cast-iron skillet over medium heat. Place onion mixture in a medium bowl and set aside. Brown sausage in skillet; drain and combine with onion mixture. Add spinach, cheeses and garlic powder; mix well. Top each egg roll wrapper with 3 tablespoons of mixture; roll up, following directions on egg roll package. Heat 3 to 4 inches oil in a deep fryer. Fry egg rolls, in batches, until golden. Drain on paper towels. Serve warm with pizza sauce for dipping.

Jennifer Niemi, Nova Scotia, Canada

Rosemary Peppers & Fusilli

This colorful, flavorful meatless side is ready to serve in a jiffy. If you can't find fusilli pasta, try medium shells, rotini or even wagon wheels.

Makes 4 servings

2 to 4 T. olive oil
2 red onions, thinly sliced and
    separated into rings
3 red, orange and/or yellow peppers,
    very thinly sliced
5 to 6 cloves garlic, very thinly sliced
3 t. dried rosemary
salt and pepper to taste
12-oz. pkg. fusilli pasta, cooked
Optional: shredded mozzarella
    cheese

Add oil to a large cast-iron skillet over medium heat. Add onions to skillet; cover and cook over medium heat for 10 minutes. Stir in remaining ingredients except pasta and cheese; reduce heat. Cook, covered, stirring occasionally, for an additional 20 minutes. Serve vegetable mixture over pasta, topped with cheese if desired.

Rosemary Peppers & Fusilli

Dutch Baby with Spiced Fruit, p. 248

CHAPTER FIVE

SIMPLE & SWEET
Desserts

Chocolate-Hazelnut Skillet Bars, p. 244   Skillet Strawberry Jam, p. 238

Barbara Cebula, Chicopee, MA

Gramma's Apple Biscuit Coffee Cake

This is a recipe handed down from my mother to me. It is very tasty with a cup of hot tea or coffee on a chilly day.

Makes 6 to 8 servings

2 T. butter, melted
2 cooking apples, peeled, cored
    and sliced
1/4 c. raisins
8-oz. tube refrigerated biscuits,
    quartered
1/4 c. brown sugar, packed
1/4 c. light corn syrup
1 egg, beaten
1/2 t. cinnamon
Optional: 1/4 c. chopped walnuts
1 T. chilled butter, diced

Spread melted butter in the bottom of a cast-iron skillet. Arrange sliced apples over butter; sprinkle raisins over apples. Arrange biscuit pieces over apples. In a bowl, mix together brown sugar, corn syrup, egg and cinnamon until well blended and brown sugar is dissolved; spoon over biscuits. Sprinkle walnuts over top, if using; dot with chilled butter. Bake at 350 degrees for 25 to 30 minutes. Invert onto a serving plate; spoon sugary juices from pan over top. Cut into wedges and serve.

Connie Patterson, San Diego, CA

Sautéed Pears

You can use any kind of pears for this dish, but the red ones are so beautiful!

Severs 8

1 T. butter
4 red pears, halved and cored
3 T. brown sugar, packed
1/4 c. dried cranberries
Garnish: pecans

In a cast-iron skillet, melt butter and add pears. Sauté for about 2 minutes, just until pears begin to soften. Add brown sugar and cranberries. Cook until tender, about 3 more minutes. Remove to plate and garnish with pecans.

FLAVOR BOOST
For just a little more zip to the pears, add 1/2 teaspoon cinnamon to the brown sugar before adding to the pan.

Sautéed Pears

Diana Bulls, Reedley, CA

Snickerdoodle Cupcakes

An easy and delicious version of an all-time favorite cookie!

Makes one dozen

18-1/4 oz. pkg. white cake mix
1 c. milk
1/2 c. butter, melted and cooled
    slightly
3 eggs, beaten
1 t. vanilla extract
2 t. cinnamon

In a large bowl, combine dry cake mix and remaining ingredients. Beat with an electric mixer on low speed for 3 minutes. Fill greased cast-iron muffin cups 2/3 full. Bake at 350 degrees for 22 to 25 minutes. Let cool. Frost with Cinnamon Frosting.

Cinnamon Frosting:
1/2 c. butter, softened
1 t. vanilla extract
1 T. cinnamon
3-3/4 c. powdered sugar
3 to 4 T. milk

Beat butter until fluffy. Mix in vanilla, cinnamon and powdered sugar. Stir in enough milk for desired consistency.

Tina Wright, Altanta, GA

Simple Skillet Peaches

These peaches are delicious on just about anything you can think of. Cereal, oatmeal, ice cream, cobbler... or use them to top big slices of angel food cake!

Makes about 6 servings

6 c. peaches, peeled, pitted and cut
    into bite-size pieces
1/2 c. sugar
1 T. vanilla extract

Combine peaches and sugar in a large cast-iron skillet over medium heat. Bring to a boil; reduce heat to medium-low. Simmer until peaches are soft and mixture has thickened, about 20 to 25 minutes. Stir in extract. Serve warm or store in an airtight container in the refrigerator.

DID YOU KNOW?
Cast-iron skillets and Dutch ovens display your food beautifully. Plan to serve your dish right from the pan resting on a pretty cloth or potholder.

Simple Skillet Peaches

Sandi Figura, Decatur, IL

Crunchy Oat & Fruit Crisp

A crunchy, fruit-filled crisp that's tasty warm or cold.

Serves 4 to 6

1 c. quick-cooking oats, uncooked
3/4 c. brown sugar, packed and
　　divided
5 T. all-purpose flour, divided
1/3 c. butter, melted
1 c. blueberries
1 c. cherries, pitted
4 apples, peeled, cored and thickly
　　sliced
1/4 c. frozen orange juice
　　concentrate, thawed
1 T. cinnamon

In a bowl, combine oats, 1/2 cup brown sugar, 2 tablespoons flour and butter. Mix until crumbly and set aside. In a separate bowl, combine fruit, remaining brown sugar and other ingredients. Stir until fruit is evenly coated. Spoon fruit mixture into a lightly buttered cast-iron skillet; sprinkle oat mixture over top. Transfer skillet to oven. Bake, uncovered, at 350 degrees for 30 to 35 minutes, until apples are tender and topping is golden.

Judy Lange, Imperial, PA

Ginger Ale Baked Apples

A yummy fall dessert or after-the-game snack!

Serves 4

4 baking apples
1/4 c. golden raisins, divided
4 t. brown sugar, packed and divided
1/2 c. ginger ale

Core apples but do not cut through bottoms. Place apples in an ungreased cast-iron skillet. Spoon one tablespoon raisins and one teaspoon brown sugar into center of each apple. Pour ginger ale over apples. Bake, uncovered, at 350 degrees, basting occasionally with ginger ale, for 45 minutes, or until apples are tender. Serve warm or cold.

Ginger Ale Baked Apples

Lisa Langston, Conroe, TX

Graham No-Bake Cookies

This is a no-bake recipe that's a little different...I've never seen this version made with graham crackers anywhere else.

Makes 4 to 5 dozen

2 c. sugar
1/2 c. milk
2 T. baking cocoa
1/2 c. butter
1/2 c. creamy peanut butter
1 T. vanilla extract
2 c. quick-cooking oats, uncooked
1 c. graham cracker crumbs

Combine sugar, milk, cocoa and butter in a cast-iron skillet over medium heat. Bring to a boil and cook for 2 minutes, stirring constantly. Remove from heat. Stir in peanut butter, vanilla, oats and crumbs; mix well. Drop by rounded tablespoonfuls onto buttered wax paper; cool completely.

Cheryl Panning, Wabash, IN

Dutch Oven Peach Cobbler

An old camping favorite. Very easy to do and the results are delicious!

Makes 6 to 8 servings

29-oz. can sliced peaches, drained
1-1/2 c. sugar, divided
1 t. butter, melted
1 c. all-purpose flour
2 t. baking powder
1/2 t. salt
1/2 c. milk
1/2 c. water

Place peaches in a greased cast-iron Dutch oven; set aside. In a bowl, mix 1/2 cup sugar and butter. In a separate bowl, mix flour, baking powder and salt. Stir flour mixture and milk into sugar mixture. Pour batter over peaches. Sprinkle with remaining sugar; pour water over batter without stirring. Cover Dutch oven with lid. Bake at 350 degrees for one hour, or until bubbly and golden. Serve warm.

Campfire Directions:
Prepare a campfire with plenty of hot charcoal briquets. Place peaches in a greased cast-iron Dutch oven; set near fire to warm. Prepare batter and add to peaches; add remaining sugar and water as described above. Arrange 7 hot charcoal briquets in a ring; set Dutch oven on top. Add lid; place 14 briquets on lid. Cook for about one hour. Every 15 minutes, carefully rotate Dutch oven 1/4 turn to the right and rotate lid 1/4 turn to the left; replace briquets on lid as needed. Cobbler is done when bubbly and golden.

Dutch Oven Peach Cobbler

Barb Lueck, Lester Prairie, MN

Peach Melba Pie

I got this recipe from my mom. It is our favorite summer pie and always makes us look forward to the warm days.

Serves 6

4 peaches, peeled, pitted and sliced
1 c. sugar
5 t. lemon juice
1/4 c. cornstarch
1/3 c. water
3 c. fresh raspberries
9-inch pie crust, baked

In a cast-iron skillet over medium heat, combine peaches, sugar and lemon juice. In a small bowl, stir cornstarch and water until smooth; stir into peach mixture. Bring to a boil; cook and stir one minute, or until thickened. Remove from heat; cool to room temperature. Gently fold in raspberries; spoon into baked pie crust. Chill at least 3 hours to overnight.

Jodi Rhodes, Tolland, CT

Whole-Wheat Pumpkin Skillet Cake

This scrumptious recipe came out of the desire for a healthier cake. For a real show-stopper, top it with freshly whipped cream.

Makes 8 servings

1/4 c. butter, sliced
1/2 c. brown sugar, packed
1 egg, beaten
1/2 t. vanilla extract
1/2 ripe banana, mashed
1/3 c. canned pumpkin
1 c. whole-wheat flour
1/2 t. baking soda
1/4 t. salt
1/2 t. cinnamon
1/4 t. nutmeg
1/2 c. chopped walnuts
1/2 c. semi-sweet chocolate chips

Melt butter in a 9" cast-iron skillet over medium heat. Remove from heat; stir in brown sugar. Let cool. Whisk in egg; stir in vanilla. Add mashed banana and pumpkin; stir until blended and set aside. In a bowl, combine flour, baking soda, salt and spices. Add to pumpkin mixture in skillet; stir until well mixed. Stir in walnuts and chocolate chips; smooth top with spoon. Bake at 350 degrees for 15 to 20 minutes. Cut into wedges to serve.

Whole-Wheat Pumpkin Skillet Cake

Nancy Willis, Farmington Hills, MI

Easy Apple Crisp

Garnish with a dollop of whipped cream and a dusting of cinnamon or an apple slice.

Serves 12

4 c. apples, cored and sliced
1/2 c. brown sugar, packed
1/2 c. quick-cooking oats, uncooked
1/3 c. all-purpose flour
3/4 t. cinnamon
1/4 c. butter
Garnish: whipped cream, cinnamon, apple slice

Arrange apple slices in a greased cast-iron skillet; set aside. Combine remaining ingredients; stir until crumbly and sprinkle over apples. Bake at 350 degrees for 30 to 35 minutes. Garnish as desired.

Tiffany Brinkley, Bloomfield, CO

Lemon Upside-Down Cake

This elegant sweet-tart cake is sure to be a hit with dinner guests.

Serves 8

4 small lemons, divided
10 T. butter, divided
3/4 c. light brown sugar, packed
1-1/2 c. all-purpose flour
1-1/2 t. baking powder
1/2 t. salt
3/4 c. sugar
1 t. vanilla extract
2 eggs
1/2 c. milk

With a sharp knife, thinly slice 3 lemons, peel and all. Discard any seeds; set aside. From remaining lemon, grate one teaspoon zest; reserve lemon for another use. In a cast-iron skillet, melt 4 tablespoons butter over medium-low heat. Brush bottom and sides of skillet with melted butter. Add brown sugar; stir well and spread evenly in skillet. Arrange lemon slices over the bottom of skillet, slightly overlapping; set aside. Combine flour, baking powder and salt in a bowl. In a separate bowl, beat remaining butter with an electric mixer on medium speed until creamy. Beat in sugar, lemon zest and vanilla until fluffy; beat in eggs, one at a time. Beat in milk and half of flour mixture. Beat in remaining flour mixture. Spread batter evenly over lemon slices in skillet. Transfer skillet to oven. Bake, uncovered, at 350 degrees for 30 to 35 minutes, until golden and center tests done with a toothpick. Cool cake in skillet on a wire rack for 5 minutes. Turn out onto a plate; cut into wedges.

Lemon Upside-Down Cake

Sara Burton, Thornville, OH

Just Peachy Blueberry Crisp

This old-fashioned crisp is always a favorite. I love to serve it with just a little whipped cream on top.

Serves 6 to 8

3 c. peaches, peeled, pitted and sliced
1/2 c. blueberries
2 t. cinnamon-sugar
1 c. all-purpose flour
1 c. brown sugar, packed
1/2 c. butter, softened
3/4 c. long-cooking oats, uncooked

Arrange peaches and blueberries in a buttered cast-iron skillet. Sprinkle with cinnamon-sugar; toss gently to coat. In a bowl, combine flour and brown sugar; cut in butter and oats with a fork until mixture is crumbly. Sprinkle mixture evenly over fruit. Bake at 350 degrees for about 40 to 45 minutes, until topping is crisp and golden. Serve warm.

Megan Brooks, Antioch, TN

Skillet Strawberry Jam

This super-simple skillet jam is delectable spread on a freshly-baked homemade biscuit or a toasty English muffin.

Makes about 1-1/2 cups

4 c. strawberries, hulled and
    crushed
1/2 c. sugar
1 T. lemon juice
Optional: 1/4 t. vanilla extract

Combine strawberries, sugar and lemon juice in a cast-iron skillet over medium high heat; mix well. Cook, stirring often, until strawberries soften and mixture thickens, about 10 minutes. Remove from heat; stir in vanilla, if using. Store in an airtight jar in refrigerator for up to 3 weeks.

DID YOU KNOW?

Cast-iron pans and Dutch ovens can be used for so many recipes. When properly seasoned, they are terrific for non-stick cooking on top of the stove as well as baking in the oven.

Skillet Strawberry Jam

Lisa Ann Panzino-DiNunzio,
Vineland, NJ

Chunky Applesauce

I love this recipe! It cooks up quickly in my favorite Dutch oven and I have it ready to serve for a quick dessert.

Makes 8 servings

10 apples, peeled, cored and cubed
1/2 c. water
1/4 c. sugar
Optional: 1 t. cinnamon

Combine all ingredients in a Dutch oven; toss to mix. Cover and cook for 30 minutes until apples are tender. Serve warm or keep refrigerated in a covered container.

Diane Axtell, Marble Falls, TX

Lemony Blackberry Crisp

The perfect reward for an afternoon spent picking blackberries!

Makes 4 to 6 servings

5 c. fresh or frozen blackberries
1/4 c. sugar
2 T. cornstarch
3 T. lemon juice
25 vanilla wafers, crushed
1/2 c. old-fashioned oats, uncooked
1/2 c. light brown sugar, packed
1/4 c. all-purpose flour
1/2 t. cinnamon
1/2 c. butter, melted
Garnish: vanilla ice cream

Place blackberries in a cast-iron Dutch oven; sprinkle with sugar and set aside. In a cup, stir together cornstarch and lemon juice; add to berries and mix gently. In a bowl, combine vanilla wafer crumbs, oats, brown sugar, flour and cinnamon. Add butter; stir until crumbly. Sprinkle crumb mixture over berries. Bake, uncovered, at 400 degrees for 25 to 30 minutes, until bubbly and lightly golden. Serve warm, topped with a scoop of ice cream.

Lemony Blackberry Crisp

Geneva Rogers, Gillette, WY

Prize-Winning Funnel Cakes

The kid in all of us loves the powdered sugar topping! Or treat yourself to a big dollop of fruit pie filling.

Makes about 4 servings

2 c. all-purpose flour
1 T. sugar
1 t. baking powder
1/4 t. salt
2 eggs, beaten
1-1/4 c. milk
oil for deep frying
Garnish: powdered sugar
Optional: apple, cherry or blueberry
    pie filling

Sift together flour, sugar, baking powder and salt into a deep bowl. Make a well in the center; add eggs and enough milk to make a thin batter. Mix well. In a cast-iron skillet, heat 2 inches oil to 375 degrees. With a fingertip over end of funnel, drop batter by 1/2 cupfuls into a funnel over hot oil, one at a time, swirling funnel as batter is released. Cook until golden, about 2 minutes per side. Drain on paper towels. Sprinkle with powdered sugar; top with pie filling, if desired. Serve immediately.

Shelley Turner, Boise, ID

Eva's Fruit Cobbler

We love the combination of rhubarb and strawberries in this yummy dessert.

Makes 8 servings

4 c. rhubarb, sliced
4 c. strawberries, hulled and halved
1 c. sugar, divided
1/4 c. water
2 T. apple juice
1 T. cornstarch
1 c. all-purpose flour
1 t. baking powder
1/4 t. baking soda
1/4 t. salt
1/4 c. butter
1/2 c. buttermilk
1/2 t. almond extract
Garnish: 2 t. coarse sugar

In a cast-iron skillet, combine fruit, 3/4 cup sugar and water; bring to a boil. Reduce heat, cover and simmer for 10 minutes. Combine apple juice and cornstarch in a container with a tight-fitting lid; shake well to blend. Stir into fruit and cook until mixture thickens. Keep warm. Combine remaining dry ingredients, including remaining sugar, in a bowl. Cut in butter with a pastry blender or 2 forks until mixture resembles crumbs. Stir together buttermilk and extract; add to dough. Stir to blend well and drop by tablespoonfuls onto hot fruit. Sprinkle with coarse sugar. Bake at 400 degrees for 20 minutes, or until golden.

Eva's Fruit Cobbler

Joanne Nagle, Ashtabula, OH

Country-Style Skillet Apples

A perfect partner for roast pork at dinner... for grilled breakfast sausages too!

Makes 4 to 6 servings

1/3 c. butter
1/2 c. sugar
1/2 t. cinnamon
2 T. cornstarch
1 c. water
4 Golden Delicious apples, cored, peeled and sliced

Melt butter in a cast-iron skillet over medium heat. Stir in sugar, cinnamon and cornstarch; mix well and stir in water. Add apple slices. Cook over medium heat, stirring occasionally, until tender, about 10 minutes.

Cheri Maxwell, Gulf Breeze, FL

Chocolate-Hazelnut Skillet Bars

These blondie-like bars are too good to pass up. If you aren't a fan of hazelnuts, pecans, almonds or even peanuts would be just as tasty!

Serves 8

1-1/4 c. all-purpose flour
1/4 t. baking powder
1/2 t. baking soda
1/2 t. salt
1/2 c. butter
1 c. dark brown sugar, packed
1 egg, beaten
1-1/2 t. vanilla extract
1 t. espresso powder
3/4 c. dark baking chocolate, chopped
1/2 c. hazelnuts, chopped

In a bowl, combine flour, baking powder, baking soda and salt; set aside. Melt butter in a large cast-iron skillet over medium heat. Add brown sugar and whisk until sugar is dissolved, about one minute. Slowly pour butter mixture into flour mixture. Add egg, vanilla and espresso powder to flour mixture; stir until combined. Fold in remaining ingredients. Spoon dough into skillet; bake at 350 degrees for 20 to 25 minutes, until golden on top and a toothpick tests clean. Let stand 30 minutes; slice into wedges to serve.

Chocolate-Hazelnut Skillet Bars

Carol Hickman, Kingsport, TN

Hot Chocolate Cupcakes

What could be better than hot chocolate? Hot chocolate muffins! You'll love them!

Makes 1-1/2 to 2 dozen

1/2 c. butter, softened
1 c. sugar
4 eggs, separated
6 T. hot chocolate mix
1/2 c. boiling water
2/3 c. milk
3 c. all-purpose flour
2 T. baking powder
1 t. salt
2 t. vanilla extract

Blend butter and sugar together in a large bowl; add egg yolks and beat until well mixed. In a separate bowl, dissolve hot chocolate mix in boiling water; add to butter mixture along with milk. Sift together flour, baking powder and salt; add to butter mixture. In a separate bowl, beat egg whites with an electric mixer on high speed until stiff peaks form; fold egg whites and vanilla into mixture. Pour into greased cast-iron cupcake pan, filling 3/4 full. Bake at 375 degrees for 20 to 25 minutes, until centers test done with a toothpick.

Brenda Derby, Northborough, MA

Apple-Cranberry Crisp

We like to make this using several different varieties of tart baking apples.

Serves 10 to 12

6 c. apples, peeled, cored and sliced
3 c. cranberries
1 c. sugar
2 t. cinnamon
1 to 2 t. lemon juice
3/4 c. butter sliced and divided
1 c. all-purpose flour
1 c. brown sugar, packed
Garnish: vanilla ice cream

Toss together apple slices, cranberries, sugar and cinnamon Spread in a greased cast-iron skillet. Sprinkle with lemon juice and dot with 1/4 cup butter. Blend remaining butter with flour and brown sugar until crumbly; sprinkle over apple mixture. Bake at 350 degrees for one hour. Serve warm with vanilla ice cream.

Apple-Cranberry Crisp

Miriam Schultz, Waukee, IA

Cale's Corn Flake Cookies

Sweet, crunchy and peanut buttery. An easy cookie recipe using pantry staples.

Makes 4 dozen

1 c. light corn syrup
1 c. creamy peanut butter
1 c. sugar
1 t. vanilla extract
6 to 7 c. corn flake cereal

In a large cast-iron skillet, combine all ingredients except cereal. Cook and stir over low heat until smooth. Add cereal; stir well. Drop by tablespoonfuls onto wax paper. Let stand until cooled and set.

Staci Prickett, Montezuma, GA

Dutch Baby with Spiced Fruit

This is an amazing recipe...everyone loves to watch it bake! It puffs up in the oven, then slightly falls when you take it out. I often make this as a late night treat when I want something a little sweet.

Makes 4 to 6 servings

3 T. butter
1/2 c. all-purpose flour
1 T. sugar
1/4 t. salt
1/8 t. nutmeg

1/2 c. milk, room temperature
2 eggs, room temperature, beaten
1 t. vanilla extract
1/8 t. lemon extract
Garnish: powdered sugar

Add butter to a cast-iron skillet; place in oven at 425 degrees to melt. In a bowl, whisk together flour, sugar, salt and spice. Stir in milk, eggs and extracts; whisk until smooth. Remove hot skillet from oven; swirl butter to evenly coat bottom of skillet. Pour batter into skillet. Bake at 425 degrees for 15 to 18 minutes, until puffy and golden on edges and spots in the center. Remove from oven. Slice and serve, topped with a spoonful of Spiced Fruit and a dusting of powdered sugar.

Spiced Fruit:
2 T. butter
4 apples and/or pears, peeled, cored
 and sliced 1/4-inch thick
1/4 c. brown sugar, packed
1 t. cornstarch
1 t. apple pie spice
2 T. lemon juice or water

Melt butter in a cast-iron skillet over medium-high heat. Add apples or pears; stir until coated with butter. Cook for about 5 minutes, until fruit begins to soften. Stir together remaining ingredients; add to skillet. Cook for another 10 minutes, stirring occasionally, or until fruit is tender and sauce has thickened. Remove from heat; let cool slightly.

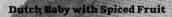
Dutch Baby with Spiced Fruit

Index

U.S. to Metric Recipe Equivalents

Volume Measurements

1/4 teaspoon.	1 mL
1/2 teaspoon	2 mL
1 teaspoon	5 mL
1 tablespoon = 3 teaspoons . . .	15 mL
2 tablespoons = 1 fluid ounce .	30 mL
1/4 cup.	60 mL
1/3 cup.	75 mL
1/2 cup = 4 fluid ounces.	125 mL
1 cup = 8 fluid ounces	250 mL
2 cups=1 pint=16 fluid ounces	500 mL
4 cups =1 quart	75 mL

Weights

1 ounce	30 g
4 ounces.	120 g
8 ounces.	225 g
16 ounces = 1 pound	450 g

Baking Pan Sizes

Square

8x8x2 inches	2 L = 20x20x5 cm
9x9x2 inches . . .	2.5 L = 23x23x5 cm

Rectangular

13x9x2 inches. . .	3.5 L = 33x23x5 cm

Loaf

9x5x3 inches	2 L = 23x13x7 cm

Round

8x1½ inches	1.2 L = 20x4 cm
9x1½ inches	1.5 L = 23x4 cm

Recipe Abbreviations

t. = teaspoon	ltr. = liter
T. = tablespoon	oz. = ounce
c. = cup	lb. = pound
pt. = pint	doz. = dozen
qt. = quart	pkg. = package
gal. = gallon	env. = envelope

Oven Temperatures

300° F	150° C
325° F	160° C
350° F	180° C
375° F	190° C
400° F	200° C
450° F	230° C

Kitchen Measurements

A pinch = 1/8 tablespoon

1 fluid ounce = 2 tablespoons

3 teaspoons = 1 tablespoon

4 fluid ounces = 1/2 cup

2 tablespoons = 1/8 cup

8 fluid ounces = 1 cup

4 tablespoons = 1/4 cup

16 fluid ounces = 1 pint

8 tablespoons = 1/2 cup

32 fluid ounces = 1 quart

16 tablespoons = 1 cup

16 ounces net weight = 1 pound

2 cups = 1 pint

4 cups = 1 quart

4 quarts = 1 gallon

Send us your favorite recipe

and the memory that makes it special for you!*

If we select your recipe for a brand-new **Gooseberry Patch** cookbook,
your name will appear right along with it...and you'll receive a
FREE copy of the book!

Submit your recipe on our website at

www.gooseberrypatch.com/sharearecipe

*Please include the number of servings and all other necessary information.

Have a taste for more?

Visit www.gooseberrypatch.com to join our Circle of Friends!

• Free recipes, tips and ideas plus a complete cookbook index
• Get mouthwatering recipes and special email offers delivered to your inbox.

You'll also love these cookbooks from **Gooseberry Patch**!

5-Ingredient Fresh Family Recipes
Classic Church Potlucks
Fast, Easy & Delicious Recipes
Grandma's Favorites
Mom's Best Sunday Dinners
**Quick & Easy Recipes with Help from My Instant Pot, Air
Fryer, Slow Cooker, Waffle Iron & more**
Our Best Recipes in a Snap
Quick & Easy Casseroles
What's For Dinner
Slow Cooking All Year 'Round
www.gooseberrypatch.com

From our Kitchen to Yours

Our Story

Back in 1984, our families were neighbors in little Delaware, Ohio. With small children, we wanted to do what we loved and stay home with the kids too. We had always shared a love of home cooking and so, **Gooseberry Patch** was born.

Almost immediately, we found a connection with our customers and it wasn't long before these friends started sharing recipes. Since then we've enjoyed publishing hundreds of cookbooks with your tried & true recipes.

We know we couldn't have done it without our

friends all across the country and we look forward to continuing to build a community with you. Welcome to the **Gooseberry Patch** family!

Jo Ann & Vickie